THE HARCOURT BRACE

GUIDE TO DOCUMENTATION AND WRITING IN THE DISCIPLINES

Fourth Edition

Laurie G. Kirszner
Philadelphia College of Pharmacy and Science

Stephen R. Mandell
Drexel University

Revised and edited by
Virginia G. Polanski
Stonehill College

with contributions from
Craig Almeida, Angelo Caranfa, Martin Curtin, Mary Joan Leith,
Annie Middleton, Joseph Puciloski, and Jennifer Swanson

HARCOURT BRACE COLLEGE PUBLISHERS
Fort Worth Philadelphia San Diego New York Orlando Austin San Antonio
Toronto Montreal London Sydney Tokyo

Acknowledgments

I acknowledge the assistance of colleagues from a variety of disciplines without whom I would not have been able to complete this project. Ken Branco—structure of the research article (Sociology); John Broderick—reviewing the Social Science section (Sociology); John Burke—chemistry lab report (Chemistry); Dan LeClair—information on the grant proposal (Criminology); Eden Fergussen—research sources for business (Reference Librarian); Theodore Jula—marketing plan outline (Marketing); Geoffrey Lantos—research sources for business (Marketing); Robert Peabody—review of Science section (Biology); Debbie Salvucci-Imbriani—review of student paper (Sociology); Robert Russell—research sources for management (Management); Maura Tyrrell—review of CBE documentation (Biology); Joseph Whitbread—research sources for finance (Finance); Russell Wilcox—research sources for computer systems management (Computer Systems Management).

Craig Almeida—model papers and completely rewritten Science section (Biology); Maria Curtin—contribution of student lab reports (Chemistry); Angelo Caranfa—contribution of student papers (philosophy) and review of library sources (Humanities); Mary Joan Leith—contribution of student papers (Religious Studies); Jennifer Swanson—review of sources in and addition of electronic sources to Business section (Business Administration); Joseph Middleton—review of research sources (Reference Librarian).

I also thank our students, who gave permission to use their papers.

On-Line Information

Most college campuses have proxy Internet servers that provide direct access to the Internet via a local area network (LAN). Internet browsers such as Netscape Navigator or Microsoft Internet Explorer are used to search the Internet for information. Searches can be conducted by typing in an address of a specific site you would like to visit. This address is called a URL. Search engines can be used to locate information on specific topics by indicating search criteria. Popular search engines include AltaVista, Infoseek, Lycos, WebCrawler, and Yahoo!.

Be aware that Web site addresses are subject to change. Be careful of original sources of Internet information.

CONTENTS

Writing in Business   225

Overview of Documentation Styles: Books   291

Overview of Documentation Styles: Articles   293

Index   295

PREPARING TO WRITE FOR RESEARCH

Identifying a Research Question or Forming a Hypothesis

In all disciplines, research is conducted to answer questions that someone wants answered. Consequently, when you as a student receive a writing assignment involving research, you must first identify the explicitly posed or the underlying question and then conduct research to answer it. The more sharply focused the question is, the more focused the response will be. If the assignment is fairly open and does not express a question, you will need to identify a question that you would like to have answered or that you think someone else would like to have answered. As you go through your notes on classwork, readings, and other sources, try to identify such a question. The answer to this question will be your paper's thesis statement.

Some scientific research begins with a question, and some begins with a tentative answer to a research question, which researchers call a hypothesis. If you begin with a question, the purpose of your research and subsequent paper will be to answer the question. If you begin with a statement that is a tentative answer to your question (a hypothesis in the sciences), the purpose of your research and paper will be to prove or disprove this statement.

Answering a Research Question or Supporting a Hypothesis

The various disciplines require you to answer your question or support your hypothesis with different types of research. Some questions, particularly those in the humanities, may be answered by library research; however, others will require methods of data collection such as field research, case studies, analyses of statistics, and questionnaires.

Once you have determined the type of research you need to conduct and either located your sources or designed your tools for data collection, you must think critically. Ask yourself how relevant, valid, and accurate your sources are. If your sources are not believable, your readers will question your credibility as a researcher and the argument you will develop. Therefore, as you choose your research materials—and later, as you take notes—you need to make judgments about the credibility of sources.

Taking Notes

Whether you are a student of humanities, social science, natural science, or business, you will find note taking an important part of preparation for writing. Once you have mastered note-taking skills, you can apply them to writing assignments in any discipline.

Whenever you have a writing assignment or anticipate getting one, determine the questions the assignment is asking or will ask you to answer. Then begin to take notes on relevant material: observations, interviews, and textbook and library readings.

For instance, when you are reading a book or article, survey it, checking the headings and subheadings in the table of contents, and especially the index, for subjects you need to read carefully or to skim. As you read, underline and annotate sources whenever possible, and then take notes on index cards. Concentrated reading can help you narrow your focus still further as you see connections among ideas and develop new perspectives. As you read and take notes, you will move toward a thesis. This thesis will answer the stated or implied question behind your assignment and become the statement that your paper will support.

Making Note Cards

Using index cards may seem cumbersome, but their advantages become obvious when you go about arranging and rearranging material. Often you do not know where you will use a particular piece of information or whether you will use it at all. You will be constantly rearranging ideas, and the flexibility of index cards makes adding and deleting information and experimenting with different sequences possible. Students who take notes in a notebook or on a tablet find that they spend as much time untangling their notes as they do writing their paper.

At the top of each card, *include a short heading* that relates the information on your card to your area of interest. Later, this heading may help you make your outline.

Each card should *accurately identify the source* of the information you are recording. These sources may be media, conversations or interviews, records, articles, or books. You need not include the complete citation, but you must include enough information to identify your source. "Wilson 72," for example, would send you back to your bibliography card carrying the complete documentation for *Patriotic Gore* by Edmund Wilson. For a book with more than one author, or for two books by the same author, you need a more complete reference. "Glazer & Moynihan 132" would suffice for *Beyond the Melting Pot* by Nathan Glazer and Daniel Patrick Moynihan. "Terkel, *Working* 135" would be necessary if you were using more than one book by Studs Terkel.

Here is one good note-card format. It illustrates notes taken from a book, but the format is applicable to all types of note taking.

Author, *Page*	Art Style & Self Image Alschuler 260	*Short* *heading*
Note	Children's view of themselves in society is reflected by their art style. A cramped, crowded art style is using only a portion of the paper shows their limited role. The society consists of home, school, and friends.	

As you take notes on note cards, you can do several things that will make the actual writing of your paper easier.

Put only one note on each card. If one card contains several different points, you will not be able to try out different ways of arranging those points.

Include everything now that you will need later to understand your note. You might think, for instance, that this makes sense:

Peyser—four important categories of new music

But in several weeks you will not remember what those four categories were. They should have been listed on your card.

Put an author's comments into your own words whenever possible. Word-for-word copying of information is probably the most inefficient way to take notes. Occasionally you will want to copy down a particularly memorable statement or the exact words of an expert on your topic, and such quotations can strengthen your paper. But in your paper, for the most part, you will summarize and paraphrase your source material, adding your own observations and judgments. Putting information into your own words now keeps you from relying too heavily on the words of others or producing a paper that is a string of quotations rather than a thoughtful interpretation and analysis of ideas.

Remember to record your own observations and reactions. As you read your sources, get into the habit of writing down all the ideas—comments, questions, links with other sources, apparent contradictions, and so on—that occur to you. If you do not, you will probably forget them. But be sure to bracket your own reactions and observations so you will not confuse them with the author's material.

Indicate what kind of information is on your note card. If you copy an author's exact words, place them in quotation marks. If you use an author's ideas but not the exact words, do not use quotation marks. (Do not forget, however, to identify your source.) Finally, if you write down your own ideas, enclose them in brackets. This system helps you avoid confusion—and plagiarism.

The student who wrote this note card was exploring the way the press portrayed President Richard Nixon during the Watergate crisis. Note that he has included only one note on his card, that both his note and its source are as complete as possible, and that he has clearly identified the first sentence as a summary ("The authors say . . .") and the other comments as his own.

```
                                    Watergate

Woodward & Bernstein 366

        The authors say that by the summer of
1973 both Alexander Haig and Henry
Kissinger urged Richard Nixon to cut his
ties with his aides. [Is there any
evidence of this? What sources support
this? Seems doubtful.]
```

Quotation Note Cards

You *quote* when you copy an author's remarks just as they appear in your source, word for word, including all punctuation, capitalization, and spelling. When recording quotations, enclose all words that are not your own within quotation marks and identify your source with appropriate documentation. Check carefully to make sure that you have not inadvertently left out quotation marks or miscopied material from your source.

```
                                    Matterhorn Accident
Whymper 393

        "Others may tread its summit-snows,
but none will ever know the feelings of
those who first gazed upon its marvelous
panorama, and none, I trust, will ever be
compelled to tell of joy turned into grief
and of laughter into mourning."
```

Paraphrase Note Cards

A *paraphrase is* a detailed restatement, in your own words, of the content of a passage. In it you not only present the main points of your source but also retain their order and emphasis as well. A paraphrase will often include brief phrases quoted from the original to convey its tone or viewpoint. When you write a paraphrase, you should present only the author's ideas and keep your own interpretations, conclusions, and evaluations separate.

You *paraphrase* when you need detailed information from specific passages of a source but not the author's exact language. For this reason paraphrase is especially useful when you are presenting technical material to a general audience. It can also be helpful for reporting complex material or a particularly intricate discussion in easily understood terms. Although the author's concepts may be essential, the terms in which they are described could be far too difficult for your readers to follow. In such cases paraphrase enables you to give a complete sense of the author's ideas without using his or her words. Paraphrase is also useful when you want to convey the sense of a section of a work of literature or a segment of dialogue.

Original: Tyndall, <u>Hours of Exercise</u> (on the advantage of using a rope while mountain climbing):

> Not to speak of the moral effect of its presence, an amount of help upon a dangerous slope that might be measured by the gravity of a few pounds is often of incalculable importance.

```
                                        Ropes
Tyndall 289

     Aside from its psychological effect,
a rope can be extremely important when a
slight steadying pressure is necessary.
```

Summary Note Cards

Unlike a paraphrase, which is a detailed restatement of a source, a summary is a general restatement, in your own words, of the meaning of a passage. Always much shorter than the original, a summary provides an overview of a piece of writing, focusing on the main idea. Because of its brevity, a summary usually eliminates the illustrations, secondary details, and asides that characterize the original. Like a paraphrase, a summary does not contain your interpretations, conclusions, or evaluations.

You summarize when you want to convey a general sense of an author's ideas to your readers. Summary is a useful technique when you want to record the main idea, but not the specific points or the exact words, of something that you have read. Because it need not follow the order or emphasis of a source, summary enables you to relate an author's ideas to your topic in a way that paraphrase and quotation do not.

```
                                        Ropes
Tyndall 289-90

     In the 1800s, climbers thought ropes
would help prevent falls by steadying
mountain climbers who had lost their
balance. However, the rope could be fatal
to all tied to it if a climber actually
fell.
```

Computer Note Taking

More and more researchers are beginning to save their notes on computer files. Sometimes this is done in the course of preparing an annotated bibliography. This task simplifies the preparation of your final paper greatly as it is often possible to copy sections from your notes into the main body of your paper. When you enter your notes into a "notes file" on computer, try to visualize your screen as an index card. Be sure to enter the complete bibliographic citation in the proper format. If you do so, you can assemble all the citations from your notes to prepare the bibliography.

Organizing Ideas

As you take notes, you need to organize your information into categories, each of which should be unified by a topic sentence that advances your argument. Each topic sentence will be supported by specific details and examples culled from your research. For instance, a sociological description of the "working mother" might provide these particulars: age 34; 81.6 percent employed with a household income of $40,000; interested in buying self-improvement, career guidance, jewelry, and beauty aids. These facts and figures can help to support a general point you may wish to make about the working mother.

Papers in all academic disciplines often include the following components.

1. An introduction in which you pose a research question and state your thesis.
2. A short review of literature, describing the work of others out of which your research question grew.
3. Evidence to support your thesis.
4. Acknowledgment of opposing points of view and an explanation of how they differ from your point of view.
5. A conclusion that restates your thesis and summarizes your research.

This general arrangement covers a wide array of papers. Suppose, for instance, you were arguing the benefits to children of having a working mother. After using an interesting anecdote or example or statistic that had appeared in a newspaper, you could state the following thesis: "Children of working mothers often develop better social skills and greater financial responsibility as a result of their experiences in child care." This thesis could be followed by a narrative paragraph describing the available information on the development of children of working mothers. You would then go on to break down your supporting argument into its major parts. After supporting each aspect of your thesis with evidence, you can present opposing points of view and show their shortcomings. Then, restate your thesis in your conclusion.

All academic disciplines rely on certain familiar patterns of organizing material. *Comparison and contrast* is one such standard method of arranging ideas. In comparison and contrast, you bring together the similarities and dissimilarities of the subjects you are writing about to support a particular statement. The following paragraph from a sociology textbook supports the statement "Mexican-Americans have faced a great deal of prejudice and discrimination" by comparing and contrasting their experiences to those of blacks and Anglos.

> Clearly Mexican-Americans have faced a great deal of prejudice and discrimination. Like blacks, Mexican-Americans were segregated in restaurants, housing, schools, public facilities, and so on. They were frequently the victims of violence, which included beatings by police and servicemen. Today, the effects of the prejudice and discrimination directed against Mexican-Americans can still be seen. For instance, they are more likely than Anglos to hold blue-collar jobs with a large number in service jobs such as janitors. Their unemployment rate averages about six points more than that for Anglos. Their median family income is only about 74 percent of the income of Anglo families. Mexican-Americans are more likely than both blacks and Anglos to experience job layoffs and cutbacks in work time. About 36 percent of the teenagers drop out of school, which is more than twice the rate for Anglo teenagers and almost double the rate for black teenagers (from Daniel M. Curran and Claire H. Renzetti, *Social Problems: Society in Crisis*, Boston: Allyn and Bacon, 1987).

Often information is organized in the order in which it occurs or in the order in which a procedure is carried out. For instance, a history paper might be organized *chronologically*, following the order in which certain historical battles were fought; a section of a scientific paper might be organized as a *process*, following the step-by-step procedure of a scientific experiment or describing a natural process such as digestion. Other familiar patterns of organizing ideas include *cause and effect* and *classification*.

Assignments in Academic Writing

Academic disciplines share certain assignments. For instance, in any discipline you may be required to write a literature survey, an abstract, or a proposal. In addition, each discipline has certain assignments—laboratory reports and case studies, for example—that are particular to it.

The most common assignments in college writing ask you to analyze a problem, a situation, or a work such as a literary text. The result is analytic papers in which you research a specific problem, gather data related to that problem, and propose specific solutions or applications of your solutions. These assignments usually require original thought, a clear statement of the problem, and suggested solutions. Most academic papers require research whether it is done in the library or the laboratory. Here is a research assignment from a marketing class.

> Provide your classmates with a list of subsidiaries owned by a parent corporation. Example: General Electric owns RCA, RCA owns Avis Car Rentals and Random House Publishers, Random House owns Harlequin, and so on. Take a survey of the major companies with which your fellow students have had negative or positive experiences, including the number of times they have dealt with a company and what the results of their dealings have been. Can you make any generalizations about major conglomerates and their subsidiaries and how they affect the ordinary consumer? Should Congress pass laws that restrict the size of the companies? Write a research paper for your congressional representative explaining why he or she should support or reject such legislation.

Here is an English assignment that requires you to research dialects of English.

> Write or tell a story about the area in which you grew up. Analyze your story to see whether you have used localized idiomatic phrases. Do your classmates understand them? Are there phrases they have used that you cannot understand? Can you define the particular dialect you are using? After doing some library research, write a paper for an audience of foreign students about how English usage varies across the United States.

Other assignments may require you to gather information about an area and its culture. For instance, in history you may be asked to gather information about the Tigua Indians; in political science you may be asked to talk to county officers or other local politicians. In these cases you will report on your findings. Writing a coherent paper requires focusing on a single idea and gathering specifics and details to support it.

Research Sources

The reference section of any library is the best place to find general research sources. The reference section of the library contains sources as diverse as encyclopedias, atlases, quotation books, and bibliographies as well as information that indicates where you actually find other material. In addition to the library's catalog, the reference section contains indexes, bibliographies, and computerized materials that can tell you where to find material on the research topic of your choice. One way to start your research is to browse in the subject section of your catalog. If you cannot find your topic in the subject section, search *The Library of Congress Subject Headings*, which lists the various names under which a subject might be listed.

General Library Sources

The following list is a guide to some of the major sources—indexes, encyclopedias, bibliographies, and other library materials that you can use to find general research information.

Indexes

Biography Index
Magazine Index
New York Times Index
Public Affairs Information Services Index
Reader's Guide to Periodical Literature
Wall Street Journal Index

Encyclopedias

Academic American Encyclopedia
Encyclopedia Americana
Encyclopaedia Britannica
The New Columbia Encyclopedia
The Random House Encyclopedia

Bibliographies

Books in Print
The Bibliographic Index

Other Sources

Dissertation Abstracts International
Editorials on File
Monthly Catalog of United States Government Publications
Encyclopaedia Britannica World Atlas
Facts on File
Statistical Abstracts of the United States
World Almanac

General Databases for Computer Searches

In many cases computerized searching makes research much faster and provides the option of combining key words (or *descriptors*) with author and title information to find exact citations. For instance, you may know only that Fredric Jameson has written an article on third-world literature, but not where it has been published or the exact title or contents. Since the article is about literature, you decide to search a literature database that yields various titles by Fredric Jameson. Matching the titles found with the key words "Third-world Literature," you find the following: Jameson, Fredric,

"World Literature in an Age of Multinational Capitalism," in *The Current in Criticism* edited by Clayton Koelb and Virgil Lokke.

Some of the most widely used general databases include the *Magazine Index, Dissertation Abstracts Online, Biography Index, Books in Print, GPO Monthly Catalog, Newsearch, National Newspaper Index, New York Times Index, Marquis Who's Who,* and the *Reader's Guide to Periodical Literature.*

It is important to remember that although many databases have a print counterpart, some are available only on-line.

CD-ROM is a rapidly expanding new technology for database searching that is available in many libraries. Many indexes that are available in a print version are now offered on CD-ROM. CD-ROM offers a cost savings over on-line database searching and more flexibility than searching print indexes.

Documenting Sources

Documentation is the acknowledgment of what you have derived from a source and exactly where in that source you found your material. Not all fields use the same style of documentation. The most widely used formats are those advocated by the Modern Language Association (MLA), *The Chicago Manual of Style* (CMS), and the American Psychological Association (APA). In addition, the sciences, engineering, and medicine have their own formats. Before writing a paper in any of these areas, you should ask your instructor what style of documentation you should use and then follow it consistently throughout your paper (See "Overview of Documentation Styles: Books," p. 291).

What to Document

You must document all materials that you borrow from your sources. Documentation enables your readers to identify your sources and to judge the quality of your work. It also encourages them to look up the books and articles that you cite. Therefore, you should carefully document the following kinds of information:

1. direct quotations
2. summaries or paraphrases of material from your sources

3. opinions, judgments, and original insights of others
4. illustrations, tables, graphs, and charts that you get from your sources

The references in your text should clearly point a reader to the borrowed material and should clearly differentiate your ideas from the ideas of your sources.

What Not to Document

Common knowledge, information that you would expect most educated readers to know, need not be documented. You can assume, for instance, that undocumented information that appears in several sources is generally known. You can also safely include facts that are widely used in encyclopedias, textbooks, newspapers, and magazines, or on television and radio. Even if the information is new to you, as long as it is generally accepted as fact, you need not indicate your source. However, information that is in dispute or that is credited to a particular person should be documented. You need not, for example, document the fact that the Declaration of Independence was signed on July 4, 1776, or that Josiah Bartlett and Oliver Wolcott signed it. However, you do have to document a historian's analysis of the document, or a particular scholar's recent discoveries about Josiah Bartlett.

As you can see, when to document is sometimes a matter of judgment. As a beginning researcher, you should document any material you believe might need acknowledgment, even if you suspect it might be common knowledge. By doing so, you avoid the possibility of plagiarism.

Summary

In general, then, in all the papers you will be asked to write in college, you will be required to express a central idea clearly and to ensure that the researched material relates to the thesis and is organized clearly. In many of the papers you will be asked to write, you will also be required to present as a central idea a well-reasoned argument, supported by research. The section that follows discusses argumentative writing.

DEVELOPING AN ARGUMENT

Arguing and Persuading

The world is filled with disagreement. One person likes pizza with anchovies; another finds anchovies disgusting. Your next-door neighbor claims the Red Sox won the World Series in 1954; you are sure they did not. One group adamantly promotes the "right to life"; another just as strongly favors the "pro-choice" stance. Each of these examples represents a difference of opinion, yet only one can be the basis for a reasoned argument requiring critical thinking.

Whether or not a person likes anchovies is a matter of personal preference. No matter how much you describe the delights of anchovies, you are not going to change the negative response of the confirmed anchovy-hater. Arguing with your neighbor who claims the Red Sox won the Series in '54 is equally fruitless. The statistics are a matter of record and can be easily discovered by checking a sports almanac. However, the question of whether abortion should remain legal can be argued rationally because it is not a simple matter of taste nor is its legitimacy a fact that can easily be discovered in a reference book. Making decisions about abortion requires weighing evidence, making judgments, and finally reaching a conclusion.

Whatever the discipline for which you are writing, neither matters of taste nor matters of fact are worthy topics for argument. Matters requiring judgments, on the other hand, may (and often should) be the subject of well-reasoned, carefully planned arguments. Consider, for example, the following article that first appeared on the editorial page of the *New York Times*.

Abortion's Grim Alternative

Jacqueline H. Plumez

Given that several Supreme Court justices are more than eighty years of age, George Bush will probably appoint enough justices during the next four years to make good his promise to outlaw most abortions. "I favor adoption," he has said. "Let them come to birth, and then put them in a family where there will be love."

Well, I favor adoption, too. For ten years, I have been researching adoption and writing positively about it. But I think that George Bush is naive to believe that adoption can replace abortion.

Outlawing abortion would unwittingly guarantee that millions of children would be raised by parents who do not want them. The price the country would pay to raise these unwanted children could financially and morally bankrupt us.

Abortion has not caused the shortage of adoptable babies. Ninety percent of adoptable infants are born out of wedlock, and today, there are 118 percent more illegitimate babies born each year than before abortion was legalized in 1973.

Furthermore, it is a false assumption that most women who are forced to bear unwanted children place them for adoption. Ninety-seven percent of unmarried women who give birth try to raise their babies themselves.

Even in the days when it was much less acceptable to be an unmarried mother, only 30 percent of the single women who gave birth placed their babies for adoption. And today, 20 percent of the women who have abortions are married women, who rarely place unwanted children for adoption.

Society and our social-welfare system are now overburdened by the number of unplanned children. It could be pushed to collapse if the current 1.6 million abortions per year become unwanted children. Twenty-three percent of America's babies are born out of wedlock—more than 878,000 illegitimate children a year. That figure could triple if abortion is criminalized.

Today, one in six teenage girls gets pregnant at least once before marriage, half of all welfare payments go to women who gave birth as teenagers, and half of all children in foster care were born out of wedlock. Studies clearly show that such mothers and children are likely to remain undereducated and live in poverty— in families that will form a huge and permanent underclass.

Contrary to George Bush's beliefs, when women give birth to unwanted children, love does not find a way. Unwanted pregnancies tend to yield unwanted children.

According to the American Psychological Association, "Unwanted childbearing has been linked to a variety of social problems, including divorce, poverty, child abuse, and juvenile delinquency. As adults, unwanted children are more likely to engage in criminal behavior, be on welfare, and receive psychiatric services."

I believe that George Bush is a kind man who wants children to grow up loved and wanted. I do too. That's why we both favor adoption. But I also believe that George Bush has not looked into the consequences of making abortion illegal. And that scares me.

Whether or not you agree with Jacqueline Plumez's view, you can see that she has argued carefully and thoughtfully to convince readers that her position is worthy of consideration. How does a writer conceive, plan, develop, draft, and revise an argument such as "Abortion's Grim Alternative"? Although we cannot know Plumez's exact process, the steps that follow explain how to write an argument, using her essay as an example.

Exploring the Issue
and Posing the Question

In college courses, whether in the humanities, the social sciences, the sciences, or business, you may be assigned a debatable position to argue for or against; or you may be assigned an issue or question and asked to formulate your own position. (In the natural sciences, this position might be called a hypothesis.) In the professional world, issues arise naturally. A supervisor, after noting the rising number of on-the-job accidents, may, for instance, write a memo arguing that the company's current safety regulations need to be changed. Nevertheless, there are also many instances when work-related writing is assigned. Plumez's editor may have said, "We need a piece on abortion." She then would have faced the same situation as a student whose professor assigns a paper on a controversial issue in literature, sociology, biology, or business.

First, she had to consider what she already knew and thought. She had to explore her previous experiences and try to identify and evaluate her emotional responses as well as her rational reactions. Plumez almost certainly had some general thoughts about the issue before she began to sort through her options, but she also knew that, like most students facing a paper assignment, she had a limited amount of space in which to present her argument, and also like students, she was facing a deadline. She certainly could not cover, or even summarize, every facet of the enormously complex abortion issue. She may have chosen at this point to jot down a list of ideas that came into her mind, topics that related to abortion. Because she had previously researched and written a great deal on adoption, the term *adoption* would be likely to appear on her list, and this may have led her to the precise, narrowed focus of her article. (See "Research Sources," pp. 10, 35, 111, 167, and 225.) Of course, any number of other scenarios are possible. For instance, she may have discussed her assignment with a friend who reminded her of her expertise on adoption. Or she may have started some preliminary reading and noticed the quotation from former President Bush that she uses in her opening paragraph. His comment may have been the spark that encouraged her to put adoption and abortion together.

As you are narrowing, refining, and defining a position for argument in any academic discipline, consider the following approaches:

1. exploratory writing (listing, note taking, or freewriting, for example)
2. collaborative discussion (with a friend, a writing center consultant, or a group of classmates)
3. preliminary reading (broadly focused reading aimed at surveying the issue rather than gathering evidence; see "Taking Notes," p. 2)

Evaluating the Audience

Once Plumez decided on a focus for her article, the connection between adoption and abortion, she had to think about the audience for whom she was writing. As a professional writer, she would know that, as a group, *New York Times* readers tend to be liberal politically and reasonably well educated. Because of their liberal bias, they are likely to be at least somewhat receptive to what she is saying. Because they are well educated, they will be able to understand the significance of statistics and will not need extended explanations of references such as the opening comment on the U.S.

Supreme Court. Plumez can make decisions about word choice, tone, and presentation of evidence based on her knowledge of her audience.

Although most papers written for a class have the instructor as the primary reader, other class members are often also part of the audience. As you consider the audience to whom you will be presenting your argument, you should ask the following questions:

1. Are my readers hostile, sympathetic, or neutral to my argument?
2. What is the education level of my readers?
3. What special knowledge of my topic can I expect from my readers?

Note: Although you present ideas differently to different audiences, you do not, of course, alter your basic stance. Once you have explored a topic thoroughly and arrived at what you believe to be the truth, you stand by your findings. What changes is the way you explain your beliefs, not the beliefs themselves.

Formulating the Thesis

Once Jacqueline Plumez had decided that she would deal with the connection between adoption and abortion, and once she had considered her audience, her next logical step was to formulate her position to answer the question: "Should abortion remain legal?" After thinking about her subject, and perhaps doing more preliminary reading and discussing (this time focusing on her specific position), she may have decided on the point expressed in the final sentence of her second paragraph ". . . George Bush is naive to believe that adoption can replace abortion." This statement, then, is her "position"; she now needs to explore evidence to see whether she can support this position with a strong argument. (See "Answering a Research Question or Supporting a Hypothesis," p. 1.)

As you formulate your position, remember that this assertion will become your thesis.

Exercise

Consider the following example.

> Issue—The number of nonreaders in the United States is in the millions and increasing.

> Question—How can elementary schools work to decrease the number of functionally illiterate citizens in the United States?

> Position (thesis)—Schools should implement President Clinton's proposal to limit class size to 18 in the primary grades and to require students to master certain skills before being promoted each year.

For each of the following topics, define an issue, pose a question, and develop a position.

> Gun-related deaths in the United States
> Noise pollution
> Child custody laws
> Capital punishment
> Health fads
> Credit ratings
> Child abuse
> Public art

Gathering Evidence

During the years Plumez researched and wrote about adoption, she almost certainly used two important thinking strategies: *inductive reasoning* and *deductive reasoning*. Anyone gathering evidence to support an argument in any discipline (but particularly in the social sciences and sciences) needs to be aware of these patterns of logical thinking.

When you explore evidence through *inductive reasoning*, as is customary in the natural sciences and in some social sciences, you observe many similar examples and then make a generalization based on what you discovered. Plumez, for example, must have observed many adoptive parents and adoptive children to have reached the conclusions that led her "to write positively about" adoption. She probably looked for specific behaviors and situations that she defined as positive and when she found them, noted the families that displayed those qualities as support for her theory.

Inductive reasoning, then, requires that you make observations of individuals and move to a general conclusion about the class to which those individuals belong. Plumez, for instance, might have moved from her observation of individual adoptive families to the general conclusion that adoption usually benefits both the adoptive parents and the child.

When you use inductive reasoning, it is important to remember these guidelines:

1. Pose a sharply focused question.
2. Observe a sufficiently large sample (interviewing two happy families—or even five or ten—would not allow for making generalizations about adoption).
3. Acknowledge and explain examples that do not support your generalization.

When you explore evidence through *deductive reasoning,* you follow a process that is just the reverse of inductive reasoning. When you use induction, you observe many examples and move to a new generalization. When you use deduction, you reason from a known principle to an unknown, from the general to the specific, or from a premise to a logical conclusion. You start with a generalization that is widely accepted and use that *assumption* as the basis for your argument. Of course, understanding your audience is very important when you write a deductive argument. In the United States, for instance, we can assume that most people value universal formal education (an assumption that is not true in some countries where school time for the lower classes is regarded as time away from the physical labor that supports poorer families' meager existence). Therefore, most readers in the United States would be willing to accept the premise that a practice that enhances education deserves consideration. Jacqueline Plumez might, then, have written a very different argument from the one that appears here. She might have begun by praising the value the United States places on universal education and then moved to a series of examples showing that unwed teenage mothers, who are more likely than other teenagers to remain uneducated, deserve that education just as much as any other legal residents. In formal terms, the argument would have looked like this:

Major premise: All legal residents of the United States are entitled to be formally educated.

Minor premise: Teenage unwed mothers discussed in this essay are legal residents of the United States.

Conclusion: Therefore, the teenage unwed mothers discussed in this essay are entitled to be formally educated.

Of course, the essay itself would not be as simple as the formal outline suggests. The deductive pattern of reasoning might lead, for example, to a conclusion suggesting ways alternative programs to educate unwed mothers could be developed.

When you use deductive reasoning, it is important to remember these guidelines:

1. The major premise must be widely accepted by your audience as true.
2. The minor premise must be widely accepted by your audience as true.
3. The reasoning used to reach your conclusion must be logically sound (for instance, in the hypothetical example above, if the author had used examples of teenage mothers who lived in Bangladesh and Bolivia, then the conclusion would not have been valid because the minor premise would have been untrue).

The discussions of inductive and deductive reasoning give examples of *primary source evidence*—that is, evidence that is discovered through personally conducted observations, investigations, or experiments. When you use primary source evidence, you must convince your readers that your findings are sound by observing the following guidelines:

1. Explain the *process* of your investigation or the *design* of your experiment when this information is needed to make your conclusions credible.
2. Be specific about the *number* of instances you observed; the larger the number, the more convincing your evidence will be.
3. Demonstrate that examples you observe are *representative* (typical) and therefore worthy to serve as the basis for general inferences and conclusions.
4. Establish your expertise or *qualifications* for carrying out the investigation or experiment.

While many arguments make use of primary source evidence, most also use *secondary source evidence*. A high percentage of papers written for the courses in the various academic disciplines require use of such evidence. (See "Research Sources," pp. 10, 35, 111, 167, and 225.) Secondary source evidence comes from researching information someone else has gathered. You may find such information through conducting interviews, through watching documentary television programs or through reading. In her essay, Jacqueline Plumez makes frequent use of secondary source evidence. For example, she cites statistics to support several of her points, and she also quotes the American Psychological Association. When you are gathering secondary source evidence, observe the following guidelines:

1. *Pay close attention and take accurate notes:* In the case of interviews, making a recording (with the permission of the person interviewed) allows you to check your notes. If you have access to a VCR, the same is true for television documentaries. (Some television stations offer transcripts of certain programs, usually for a small fee.) With library periodicals or books, making one photo copy of a page or two provides you with the option for a final accuracy check. Material from the World Wide Web can be printed to facilitate use.

2. *Evaluate the expertise and possible biases of your sources:* You must be certain that individuals whose ideas you cite to support your arguments are respected in their fields, even by those who disagree with their views. For instance, William F. Buckley, Jr., a conservative writer, has a solid reputation among people with widely divergent political views. A quotation from Buckley would certainly carry far more authority (even with someone who disagreed with him politically) than one from a writer in the *National Enquirer,* which is known for its sensational and highly inaccurate reporting. And even respected writers may have personal biases that are widely known and that therefore make their ideas less convincing than the views of a more objective source. Students conducting searches on the Web must be especially careful about checking the authority of authors of material the find there.

3. *Evaluating the accuracy of the information you gather:* A helpful way to evaluate accuracy is to consult more than one source on the same topic. If several sources confirm the same findings and report the same statistics (and if these sources are all well respected), you can be fairly certain the data you want to use are correct. Some statements, of course, cannot be tested for absolute accuracy, but you should weigh their validity by considering logical fallacies and assuring yourself that none of the writers you plan to cite has been guilty of fallacious reasoning.

Drafting the Argument

Once you have gathered and evaluated your evidence, you then decide whether or not you can convincingly support your tentative thesis. If you cannot, you have two choices: You can modify or even discard your thesis (remember that the primary point of an argument is to discover and reveal the truth), or, if you believe that your thesis is valid, you can seek more evidence that you think will persuade your readers. When you have finally finished gathering evidence, you must decide how to use it most effectively in your written argument. Generally, evidence makes up the body of the argument whereas the introduction and conclusion serve other purposes. For this reason, many writers draft the body of their essay first and then work on their introduction and conclusion.

Understanding the primary purposes of each part of an argument provides a helpful overview of the process of writing a persuasive essay.

Introduction

The introduction of an argument may be a single paragraph or, as in Jacqueline Plumez's article, it may be composed of several paragraphs. In the opening section, you want to get your reader's attention, perhaps by using a significant quotation (as Plumez does). You also want to establish your credibility. Although not all arguments allow for the use of first person, when possible it is extremely useful to demonstrate your expertise in an area as Plumez does when she says, "For ten years, I have been researching adoption and writing about it positively." With this statement, she also suggests that she is not unfairly biased against adoption and that, in fact, she favors the process. Plumez does everything she can to establish a believable *persona*—that is, to demonstrate a writing personality her audience will see as thoughtful, rational, and fair-minded. As a writer develops a credible "self," he or she strives in the opening paragraphs of arguments to establish *common ground* (a body of shared assumptions) with the audience. By explaining her agreement with Bush on adoption, Plumez also aligns herself with those readers (the vast majority) who believe that adoption is a positive social institution. When readers hold values in common with a writer, they are more likely to listen to that writer with an open mind. In addition to capturing readers' interest and creating a favorable self-image, the opening of an argument should also suggest its direction. When Plumez says, "I think that George Bush is naive to believe that adoption can replace abortion," she indicates that her essay will argue for maintaining the legalization of abortion and that it will focus specifically on problems with the proposal that adoption replace abortion.

Body

How you organize the body of your essay depends on several factors. (See "Organizing Ideas," p. 7.) One of the first choices you must make concerns whether you want to deal with *opposing claims* early in your essay, integrate them throughout your essay, or treat them in your conclusion. Plumez structures her essay by challenging opposing claims, offering evidence to support her challenges, and then establishing her own claims. First she discusses why adoption cannot be a replacement for abortion, offering statistics regarding illegitimate births and the behavior pattern of unwed mothers to explain her contention that abortion has not caused the shortage of adoptable babies. Only after she has dealt with the opposing claim concerning adoption does she provide additional reasons why she believes abortion must not be criminalized. Plumez's article, then, provides one possible pattern for the body of an argument:

1. Explain and refute opposing claims.
2. Introduce new evidence.

You may, instead, choose a different pattern. Consider, for example, these two possible variations:

1. Introduce and support your first point; explain and refute any claim opposing that point.
2. Introduce and support your second point; explain and refute any claim opposing that point.

or

1. Introduce and support all of your points.
2. Explain and refute opposing claims.

Sometimes, of course, your opponents have legitimate claims. In that case, you may choose to briefly acknowledge those points but move on quickly to show that those few legitimate claims do not validate the opponents' entire argument. Plumez, for instance, notes that Bush's pro-adoption stand is admirable, but she moves on to explain why that belief does not lead logically to his stand on abortion.

Argumentative papers in all academic disciplines require you to decide where and how you will refute opposing claims. In addition, you must also make other decisions about ordering evidence. For example, will you offer your strongest points first, hoping to win converts to your cause as soon as possible, or will you save the most important evidence for a powerful conclusion, hoping to leave readers with the point you consider most crucial firmly in mind? Neither decision is necessarily right or wrong, but it is certainly essential to evaluate your evidence so that you understand your strong points as well as your weaker points and use them to what you believe will be the best advantage.

You must also decide whether your argument will appeal primarily to the minds *(appeals to reason)* of your readers, or primarily to their feelings *(appeals to emotion)* or whether you will try to sway both their thoughts and their feelings. (Sometimes the term *persuasion* is applied to appeals primarily to emotions while *argument* is used to describe appeals to the mind. In reality, most essays in any discipline that aim to reveal what the writer believes to be true and to convince others to accept those ideas as true combine rational and emotional appeals.) Although emotional appeals are often thought of as somehow less worthy and less important than rational appeals, the two are usually equally powerful and equally deserving of consideration. We are, after all, human beings, and one important sign of our humanity is that we make choices based on our feelings as well as our thoughts. Of course, both rational and emotional appeals must be presented honestly. No one likes to feel duped, and if the members of your audience realize, for example, that you have manipulated statistics to appeal falsely to their minds, they will be just as disillusioned as they would be if you created exaggerated pictures of misery to incite their horror or fear with no purpose other than to gain profit (or power) for yourself. As you draft the body of your argument, stay aware of your appeals and make sure they are both valid and balanced. You do not want to project the image of an unthinking automaton who simply spits out charts and figures, but neither do you want to seem hysterical, shrill, or morbid.

Conclusion

Just as the introduction is worthy of concentrated effort and attention because it provides your readers with their first impression of you and your argument, your conclusion, too, must be carefully planned because it leaves the final image in your audience's mind. Although you may be tempted to simply summarize the points you have made in the body of your argument, it is usually wise to resist this temptation. Particularly if your argument is relatively short, your audience should be able to remember your main ideas as well as at least some of the evidence you have provided for support. In your final paragraphs, then, you want to offer something more than a simple review. Consider, for example, Plumez's last three paragraphs. First, she returns to her opening reference to George Bush, once again refuting his claim, yet doing it in a different way than she did in her introduction. She follows up her contention that "unwanted pregnancies tend to yield unwanted children" with a quotation from the American Psychological Association that projects distinctly undesirable effects of forced childbearing. Here Plumez does not simply restate earlier evidence suggesting that problems will occur for single mothers and for our social-welfare system if abortion is criminalized; instead she offers a final, powerful look at the probable fate of the unwanted who will be born. If she has any chance of convincing her audience to accept her views, this argument should be the most effective. Even people who are unconcerned with the fate of unwed mothers or the burdening of the social-welfare system may very well be moved by the picture of children doomed to grow up in the shadow of "poverty, child abuse, and juvenile delinquency." In her final paragraph, Plumez once again shows herself to be a rational, calm writer with no personal grudge against Mr. Bush: "I believe that George Bush is a kind man," she says. And when she adds that he is a person "who wants children to grow up loved and wanted," and that she does, too, she once again establishes common ground not only with Bush, but also with most readers who will certainly share those values. Only after this demonstration of mutual beliefs and only after a confirmation of her belief in adoption does Plumez go on to her controversial final statements: "But I also believe that George Bush has not looked into the consequences of making abortion illegal. And that scares me." She hopes, of course, that the evidence she has offered earlier in the essay will lead at least some of her readers to share her concern and her fear and to agree with her argument that abortion must remain legal.

When you are writing the conclusion of an argument, remember these guidelines:

1. Make certain your final comments follow logically from and are supported by the evidence you have provided in the body of your essay.

2. Consider various approaches for leaving a strong, final impression on your audience. For example, you might include

    • a relevant and memorable quotation
    • an especially convincing example or piece of evidence
    • a compelling statistic
    • a moving anecdote

3. Be sure that your conclusion does more than summarize; it should also evaluate, analyze, predict, or recommend.

4. Reaffirm your stance as a reasonable, thoughtful writer.

Revising the Argument

Drafting an argument does not, of course, assure that you have produced a finished copy. In most cases, the draft simply provides you with workable material that you must mold into the best possible essay to support your thesis and to convince your readers of its validity.

As you begin the revising (literally, the "re-seeing") process, one of the most effective—yet most difficult—approaches is to try to take on the feelings and thoughts of a hostile reader. Even though the audience for whom you are writing may be neutral or may favor your thesis, you will see the weak spots more quickly if you adopt the mindset of those who most adamantly oppose your argument. Since you have already researched opposing claims, you know some of the main points your opponents would make, but you have to go further. Now you have to imagine someone who does not agree with you, someone who is reading and responding to what you have written. How might that person attack your evidence? Can you anticipate his or her counterarguments? And, of course, most important, can you make any changes in your essay that will block those attacks or counterarguments?

Consider, for example, Jacqueline Plumez's article, which has been used to demonstrate strategies for writing strong arguments. Here is a finished, published piece, yet even so there are questions opponents might raise. As a quick exercise in revision, reread "Abortion's Grim Alternative" and note objections you might raise or challenges you might make. For instance, in paragraph four, Plumez notes that 118 percent more illegitimate babies are now born out of wedlock than were in 1973, when abortion was legalized. Later in her essay she argues that abortion must remain legal in order to stop the number of illegitimate births. An opponent might ask Plumez whether she did not see a contradiction here. Since illegitimate births have *increased* following the legalizing of abortion, how can she suggest abortion as a solution? And how might Plumez have avoided that challenge if she had anticipated it? She might have noted that she was not proposing abortion as the only solution, or the best solution, to illegitimate births but that criminalizing abortion would certainly complicate the problem. Whether you agree or disagree with Plumez, your rereading no doubt led you to see other statements that her opponents might challenge. Are there ways Plumez could have changed her essay to answer those challenges? Or was she wise to ignore them and continue presenting her own evidence? Obviously no writer can provide minute explication of every piece of evidence; part of the revision process requires deciding where more explanation will strengthen what you have written and where more explanation will simply confuse or annoy the reader.

One question you may raise when evaluating Plumez's essay is, why does she not fully document her sources? (See "Documenting Sources," p. 12.) She cites many statistics and quotes both former President Bush and the American Psychological Association, but she does not tell readers where she found this information. Every English course from elementary school through the graduate level teaches the importance of proper documentation, yet Plumez's article is typical of those published in newspapers and popular magazines. The answer to your question about documentation lies in the varying conventions of popular journalism and academic publishing. Papers that are written for classes or for scholarly journals require careful identification of sources for three reasons: Readers can evaluate the probable validity of your evidence by knowing its source, readers can consult your sources for further information or to examine the data in context, and readers can recognize your acknowledgment of using data compiled by others. Especially in an academic setting, acknowledging sources is essential to avoid the charge of plagiarism. (For proper documentation format, see "Documentation Formats," pp. 42, 120, 174, and 233.) Remember that different disciplines use different forms; check with your instructor to learn which you should follow.

As you revise an argumentative essay, consider the following guidelines:

1. Make certain your introduction catches the reader's attention and establishes the thesis of your argument.
2. Make certain you have organized your evidence effectively.
3. Make certain you have provided sufficient evidence to make your case convincing.
4. Make certain statistics and other data are accurate and are derived from respected sources.
5. Make certain you have not used unfounded emotional appeals.
6. Make certain your rational appeals are logical and valid (check your writing handbook).
7. Make certain you have anticipated and defused opposing claims.
8. Make certain you have established a credible writing persona.
9. Make certain your conclusion follows logically from the evidence you have presented.
10. Make certain you have proofread carefully.

Topics for Argumentative Writing

You will develop most arguments in response to a specific assignment or situation. The following list provides representative topics from various academic disciplines.

The Humanities

1. Consider three important decisions Lincoln made during the Civil War and present an argument explaining why you think those decisions did or did not prolong the war unnecessarily.
2. During World War II, press photographers were censored and were not allowed to show the full horror through pictures of dismembered bodies and other such results of battle. During the Korean and Vietnam conflicts such censorship was not in place. After investigating this issue, argue for the policy you favor.
3. Should freedom of speech include the right to burn the American flag? Is this a topic worthy of congressional debate and possibly a constitutional amendment? After reading the claims of people on both sides of this issue, write an argument defending your point of view.

The Social Sciences

4. Many state governments support a lottery. Does this legalization of gambling represent a threat to the moral fabric of those states' citizens? Are state lotteries, in fact, encouraging false hopes and, worse, providing a breeding ground for the disease of compulsive gambling? Study the issue and offer an argument explaining your point of view.
5. Recent surveys suggest that many high school graduates do not know basic facts of geography, history, or literature, nor can they do simple math problems. Should nationwide "exit exams" be required, to assure that all high school graduates have acquired a certain degree of "cultural literacy"? Investigate this topic and argue for the conclusion you reach.
6. Experts on childhood development disagree concerning the benefits of organized sports teams that begin with players as young as age 5. Investigate the physical as well as psychological benefits and detriments of organized sports for young children. Then write an essay arguing for or against participation on such teams.

7. Corporations are obligated to provide paternity leave as well as maternity leave. After researching this topic, argue for or against compensated leave time for new fathers.

The Sciences

8. Some scientists have argued that the declining rate of childbearing among educated women will lead to a decline in the intelligence and productivity of the U.S. population. Do you agree? Investigate this question and then write an argument explaining your response.
9. What policies has your state implemented to address environmental concerns? Investigate this question and then decide whether or not you think the actions taken are sufficient. Write an argument defending your view.
10. Recent court cases show that patients and their families are increasingly seeking the right to make their own decisions about the use of life-support systems to sustain hopelessly terminal cases. Who should make the decision? Patients and/or their families? A judge? A doctor? After investigating this issue, write an argument explaining your recommendations.

A Final Note

In many of the papers you will be asked to write in college, you will be required to present a well-reasoned argument and to ensure that researched material supports that argument in a clearly identifiable pattern. However, each of the four broad disciplinary areas—the humanities, the social sciences, the sciences, and business—has its own particular research sources, paper formats, assignments, styles, and methods of documentation. The sections that follow discuss the differences in the four disciplinary areas.

WRITING IN THE HUMANITIES

The humanities include a variety of subjects, among them art, music, literature, history, languages, and philosophy. Some of these disciplines use different documentation styles and special library sources.

Research Sources

Library research is an important part of study in many humanities disciplines. When you begin your research in any subject area, the *Humanities Index* is one general source you can turn to. There are also many specialized sources available as you continue your research process.

Specialized Library Sources

The following list represents some of the sources used often in the various humanities disciplines.

Art

> *Art Index*
> *Dictionary of Art*
> *Fine Arts: A Bibliographic Guide to Reference Works,*
> *Histories and Handbooks*
> *Oxford Companion to Art*

Drama

> *Cambridge Guide to World Theatre*
> *McGraw-Hill Encyclopedia of World Art*
> *New York Times Theatre Reviews*
> *Oxford Companion to Art*

Film

Film: A Reference Guide
Film Literature Index
Guide to Critical Reviews
New York Times Film Reviews

History

America: History and Life
Guide to Historical Literature
Harvard Guide to American History
Historical Abstracts (Europe)

Language and Literature

Contemporary Authors
LLBA (Language and Language Behavior Abstracts)
MLA International Bibliography
Oxford English Dictionary

Music

Grove's Dictionary of Music and Musicians
Harvard Dictionary of Music
Music Index

Philosophy

The Concise Encyclopedia of Western Philosophy
  and Philosophers
Encyclopedia of Philosophy
Philosopher's Index

Specialized Databases for Computer Searches

Many of the print indexes that appear on the above list of specialized library sources are also available on-line or on CD-ROM databases. Some of the most helpful databases for humanities disciplines include *Humanities Index, Art Index, MLA Bibliography, Religion*

Index, Philosopher's Index, RILM Abstracts, Essay and General Literature Index, Artbibliographies Modern, Historical Abstracts, the *LLBA Index,* and *Comprehensive Dissertation Abstracts.*

The World Wide Web (WWW) offers a wealth of information; however, since anyone can put anything on the Web, students must be careful to check the credibility of the authors of Web site information.

The following Web sites should lead to reliable sources. Notice that these are maintained and updated by universities and organizations that control the quality of the information which they list. The individual sites are subject to change.

American studies:
<http://www.georgetown.edu/crossroads/asw/lit.html>

Arts:
<http://www.artsnet.org/Artsites/Artsites.html>
<http://witcombe.bcpw.sbc.edu/ARTHLinks.htmI >

English:
<http://www.english.upenn.edu/-jlynch/Lit/>
<http://english-www.hss.cmu.edu/>

History:
<http://www.tntech.edu/www/acad/hist/period.html>
<http://www.tntech.edu/www/acad/hist/subject.html>

Humanities:
<http://www.lib.Isu.edu/weblio.html#Humanities>
< http://humanitas.ucsb.edu/>

International Studies:
<http://www.pitt.edu/~ian/ianres.html>
<http://www.law.ecel.uwa.edu.au/intlaw/>

Music:
<http://www.music.indiana.edu/music_resources/>
<http://www.siba.fi/Kulttuuripalvelut/music.html>

Philosophy and religion:
<http://web.bu.edu/STH/Library/contents.html>
<http://humanities.uchicago.edu/humanities/philosophy/
    p-index.html>

Nonlibrary Sources

Research in the humanities is not limited to the library. Historians may need to do oral interviews or archival work or consult papers collected in town halls, churches, or courthouses. Art majors may need to visit museums and galleries. Attending concerts is a legitimate form of field work for music majors.

Nonlibrary sources can be important additions to a paper in any humanities discipline. For instance, in writing about history you not only study the events of the past, but you also interpret the information you collect. It is then up to you to defend your interpretation of those events. The following excerpt from a student's oral history interview was a valuable resource for her paper about Tigua Indians.

> Arturo Tapia, a registered Tigua Indian, recalls, "My daddy never used to say he was Tigua Indian . . . we never talked about it . . . other Indians never liked us and the white people never allowed us in their bars or stores. I have gone up to people and told them I am Tigua and they say, 'What a low class Indian,' or 'Them down there, the Mexicans, they sold out.'"

The student who recorded this interview chose to use it in her opening paragraph, to help introduce her paper's thesis.

> The history of the Tiguas is full of misconceptions. The New Mexico version of the Tiguas' migration is that they fled with a Spanish party to El Paso during the Indian uprising of August 10, 1680, while the Tigua version of their migration is quite different. The New Mexico Indians have portrayed the Tiguas of Isleta as a "Judas Tribe" who turned against their own people to ally with the Spanish. Even today the Tiguas face discrimination from other Indians as well as from Whites and feel they are considered "low class" (Rosario).

Assignments in the Humanities

The Response Statement

One assignment particular to the humanities is the response statement, in which you analyze and interpret your reactions to a work. In such a paper you are asked simply to express your personal reaction to a work such as Keats's "Ode to a Grecian Urn" or to a painting or to a concert you attended. Such an assignment requires you to write a first-person account of your feelings upon encountering a work and to account, if you can, for what influenced your response.

The Book Review

A book review summarizes or outlines a book and provides your evaluation of it. Book reviews are assigned in all the humanities disciplines, particularly literature, history, and philosophy, and in most cross-disciplinary humanities or general education sequences. Here is a sample book review from *World Literature Today,* Spring 1988.

> Timothy Mo's novel *An Insular Possession* is a rather slow-moving account of British colonizers in the Far East. . . . Walter Eastman, one of the principal characters, calls himself, in a letter, a "philosopher of the verandah." Even the American characters are infected with British practices, as they are with loathing for their steamy surroundings and the natives.
>
> What Mo does do beautifully is evoke that languid, steamy existence. In his delicate and beautifully written descriptions he shows the power of the English language in the hands of non-native English-speaking ex-colonials. His characters O'Rourke and Eastman are painters, metaphors for the author himself as he paints with delicate strokes these lives lived under muslin nets and the East as seen out of these nets.

The Art Review

Art reviews are similar to book reviews in that they assess the worth of a work of art or of an artist. Here is an excerpt from "Tom Mulder: Painting Indians" in *Utah Holiday,* October 18, 1976.

> I stand before a picture in Phillips Art Gallery in Salt Lake City, Utah. Suddenly home (India) is vividly alive. It spreads beyond the canvas and encapsulates me. I can feel the rhythm of the movements, as three women carry brass pots on their heads and can hear the clinking of their anklets. With his view of both cultures, Southwestern American and subcontinental Asian, Mulder feels one could transport a subcontinental village to the American Southwest, take an Indian posture and make of it a Navajo. The American Southwest of these paintings feels curiously like home. The color, the light are essentially the same; and yet the rugweaver is a Navajo. An artist seeing similarities between two types of "Indians"?

The Bibliographic Essay

A bibliographic essay surveys research in the field and compares and contrasts the usefulness of various sources on a particular subject. Several publications in the humanities publish bibliographic essays on a yearly basis to inform scholars of the current developments in the field. Here, for example, is a short excerpt from the "Pound and Eliot" chapter of *American Literary Scholarship.*

> This has been a good year for theoretical work on Pound. Martin A. Kayman connects Pound's theory of the image to his theory of money in "Ezra Pound: The Color of His Money" (*Paideuma* 15, ii–iii:39–52). I find Kayman's argument here interesting but problematic in his unexamined assumption that Pound never changed, that the aesthetics of 1912–14 are the same as the politics of the 1930s. That is explicitly the argument of an unintelligent essay by Robert Lumsden, "Ezra Pound's Imagism" (*Paideuma* 15, ii–iii:253–64) who argues that Pound remained an imagist and that there is no significant distinction between image, vortex, ideoplasty and ideogram.

Note that in a bibliographic essay the author must include both his or her assessment of the work at hand and the full citation of the source. This differs from the annotated bibliography in which, in the annotation or the summary assessment, you try not to interject a personal point of view and do not include the author's name, the work's title, or publication information within the summary itself.

The Annotated Bibliography

Each entry in an annotated bibliography includes the full citation of a reference source and a short summary or abstract of the source. The abstract should be a distilled, factual summary; brevity is important. Try not to include any material from the citation in the text of the abstract. For example:

> Stead, C. K. *Pound, Yeats, Eliot and the Modernist Movement.* New Brunswick: Rutgers University Press, 1986.

> Stead's overall theses are as follows: (1) Pound and Eliot are central modernists; Yeats is not; and (2) Pound's politics are less distasteful than Eliot's because Pound at least had the courage of his convictions. The value of the book lies in Stead's close readings of many poems by Pound, Eliot, and Yeats. This general thrust is to show Eliot's deep influence on Pound in matters of form and technique.

Conventions of Style and Format

The humanities paper is a single unit in which all the paragraphs are connected to the thesis and to one another. Although papers may include internal headings and abstracts, they rarely do so. Writing in the humanities can be less formal than in the social sciences and sciences and may be directed at a lay audience. Note, for example, how much less formal the art review is than the other examples of common assignments. The book review is descriptive and evaluative while the bibliographic essay is more precise. Notice that the entry for the annotated bibliography is most concise and specific. Clarity and restraint from the overuse of jargon are important considerations. Writing in the first person is acceptable when you are expressing your own reactions and convictions. In other cases, however, you should use an objective tone and write in the third person (he, she, it).

In writing papers for literature, certain conventions of literary analysis are required. You may need to analyze the way a work is constructed. For example: Is it a novel that relies heavily on flashbacks? How does that structure affect the author's purpose or theme? As points of entry into literary analysis you can look at subjects such as plot, characterization, theme, the use of imagery, and the writer's style. Literary analysis can be formal, historical, psychoanalytical, or economic. Keep in mind that it is not possible to concern yourself with all of these issues in one paper. You need to decide on one approach and one point of view and then develop that point of view in your paper.

Documentation Formats

As in all other disciplines, most of the subject areas in the humanities use documentation formats particular to the subject. English and modem and classical language scholars use the MLA format; art, history, music and philosophy scholars use *The Chicago Manual of Style*. Researchers in linguistics and languages use the *Handbook of the Linguistics Society of America* and sometimes the APA format used by the social sciences. (See p. 120 for information on the APA style.)

The MLA Format*

The MLA format is recommended by the Modern Language Association of America, a professional organization of more than 25,000 teachers of English and other languages. It is required by teachers in the humanities at colleges throughout the United States and Canada. This method of documentation has three parts: parenthetical references in the text, a list of works cited, and content notes. Full sample papers illustrating the MLA format begin on pages. A detailed description of this format can be found on-line at <http//www.mla.org/main_stl.htm>.

*MLA documentation Information format follows the guidelines set in the *MLA Handbook for Writers of Research Papers*, 4th ed. (New York: MLA, 1995) and updated in the *MLA Style Manual and Guide to Scholarly Publishing* (New York: MLA, 1998).

Parenthetical References in the Text

MLA documentation uses references inserted in parentheses within the text and keyed to a list of works cited at the end of the paper. A typical reference consists of the author's last name and a page number.

```
The   colony's  religious  and  political  freedom
appeared to many idealists in Europe (Ripley 132).
```

A reference to an electronic source may include paragraph numbers(s) rather than page number(s). If you use more than one source by the same author, shorten the title of each work to one or two key words and include the appropriate shortened title in the parenthetical reference.

```
Penn emphasized his religious motivation
(Kelley, William Penn 116).
```

If you state the author's name or the title of the work in your sentence, do not include it in the parenthetical reference. Only a page reference is necessary.

```
Penn's   political   motivation   is   discussed   by
Joseph  P.  Kelley  in  Pennsylvania,  The  Colonial
Years, 1681-1776 (44).
```

Keep in mind that you punctuate differently with paraphrases and summaries, quotations incorporated into the text, and quotations that are set off from the text.

Parenthetical documentation for *paraphrases* and *summaries* should appear *before* terminal punctuation marks.

```
Penn's   writings   epitomize   seventeenth-century
religious thought (Degler and Curtis 72).
```

Parenthetical documentation for *quotations run in with the text* should appear *after* the quotation marks but *before* the terminal punctuation.

```
As Ross says, "Penn followed his conscience in
all matters" (127).
```

```
We must now ask, as Ross does, "Did Penn follow
Quaker dictates in his dealings with Native
Americans" (128)?
```

```
According to Williams, "Penn's utopian vision was
informed by his Quaker beliefs . . ."(72).
```

Parenthetical documentation for *quotations that are set off from the text* should appear two spaces *after* the final punctuation.

```
. . . a commonwealth in which all individuals can
follow God's truth and develop according to God's
will. (Smith 314)
```

Note: Quotations set off from the text take no quotation marks.

Sample References

Parenthetical references are a straightforward and easy way to provide documentation. Here are the forms required in some special situations.

Works by more than one author

```
One group of physicists questioned many of the
assumptions of relativity (Harbeck and Johnson
31).
```

```
With the advent of behaviorism, psychology began
a new phase of inquiry (Cowen, Barbo, and Crum
31-34).
```

For works with more than three authors, list the first author followed by *et al.* ("and others") in place of the rest.

```
A number of important discoveries were made off
the coast of Crete in 1960 (Dugan et al. 63).
```

Two or more works by the same author

To cite two or more works by the same author, include the author's last name and a comma; the complete title, if it is brief, or a shortened version; and the page reference. Thus, two novels by Saul Bel-low, *Seize the Day* and *Henderson the Rain King*, would be cited `(Bellow, Seize the Day 43)` and `(Bellow, Henderson 89)`.

Works with a volume and page number

If you list more than one volume of a multivolume work in the Works Cited list, include the appropriate volume and page number, separated by a colon.

```
In 1912 Virginia Stephen married Leonard Woolf,
with whom she founded Hogarth Press (Woolf 1:
17).
```

If you use only one volume of a multivolume work and have in-cluded the volume number in the Works Cited list, include just the page number in the parenthetical reference (Woolf 17).

Works without a listed author

For works without a listed author, use a shortened version of the title in the parenthetical reference.

```
Television ratings wars have escalated during the
past ten years ("Leaving the Cellar" 102).
```

A work that is one page long

Omit the page reference if you are citing a one-page article.

```
It is a curious fact that the introduction of
Christianity at the end of the Roman Empire "had
no   effect   on   the   abolition   of   slavery"
("Slavery").
```

Indirect sources

Indicate that material is from an indirect source by using the abbre-viation *qtd. in* ("quoted in") as part of the parenthetical reference.

```
Wagner said that myth and history stood before
him "with opposing claims" (qtd. in Winkler 10).
```

More than one work within a single set of parentheses

You may cite more than one work within a single set of parentheses. Cite each work as you normally would, separating one from another with semicolons.

```
The Brooklyn Bridge has been used as a subject by
many American artists (McCullough 144; Tashjian
59).
```

Whenever possible, present long references as content notes (see page 59).

Two authors with the same last name

When two of the authors you cite in your paper have the same last name, include the initials in your references. For example, references in the same paper to Wilbert Snow's "The Robert Frost I Knew" and C. P. Snow's "The Two Cultures" would be (Snow, W. 37) and (Snow, C. P. 71).

Literary works

In citations of prose works, it is often helpful to include more than just author and page number. For example, the chapter number of a novel enables readers to locate your reference in any edition of the work to which you are referring. In parenthetical references to prose works, begin with the page number, followed by a semicolon, and add any additional information that might be necessary.

```
In Moby-Dick, Melville refers to a whaling
expedition funded by Louis XIV of France (151;
ch. 24).
```

In parenthetical references to poems, separate the divisions and line numbers with periods. Titles of books in the Bible are often abbreviated (Gen. 5.12). In the following citation, the reference is to book 8, line 124 of the *Aeneid*.

```
Virgil describes the ships as cleaving the "green
woods reflected in the calm water" (Aeneid,
8.124).
```

An entire work

When citing an entire work rather than part of a work, include just the author's last name in the text of your paper. If you wish, you may mention the author's name in a parenthetical reference.

```
Northrup Frye's Fearful Symmetry presents a
complex critical interpretation of Blake's
poetry.

Fearful Symmetry presents a complex critical
interpretation of Blake's poetry (Frye).
```

Tables and illustrations

When citing tables and illustrations, include the documentation below the illustrative material.

```
Miscues which alter meaning      51%
Overall loss of comprehension    40%
Retelling score                  20%


Source: Alice S. Horning, The "Trouble with
Writing Is the Trouble with Reading" Journal of
Basic Writing 6 (1987): 46.
```

The List of Works Cited

Your parenthetical references are keyed to a *Works Cited* section that lists all the books, articles, interviews, letters, films, and other sources that you use in your paper. If your instructor wants you to include all the sources you consulted, whether you actually cite them or not, use the title *Works Consulted*.

Arrangement of citations

Your *Works Cited* section should begin on a new, numbered page after your last page of text. For example, if the text of your paper ends on page 7, then your *Works Cited* list will begin on page 8. The heading *Works Cited* should be centered one inch from the top of the paper. Double-space and begin each entry flush with the left-hand margin. Subsequent lines of the entry should be indented one-half inch (or five spaces if you are using a typewriter) from the left-hand margin. Double-space within and between entries.

In general, entries are arranged alphabetically, according to the last name of each author or to the first word of the title if the author is not known. Articles—*a, an,* and *the*—at the beginning of a title are not considered first words.

Capitalize the first words, last words, and all important words of the title. Do not capitalize articles, prepositions introducing phrases, coordinating conjunctions, and the *to* of infinitives (unless such words are the first or last words of the title). To conserve space, use a shortened form of the publisher's name, and do not include words such as *Incorporated, Company,* or *Publishers* after the name of the publisher. Thus *Holt, Rinehart and Winston* and *Oxford University Press, Inc.* become *Holt* and *Oxford UP.* When a publisher lists offices in several cities, give only the first; for cities outside the United States, add the abbreviation for the country if the city would be ambiguous or unfamiliar to readers (Birmingham, Eng., for example).

Sample Citations: Books

If you are citing books, your entries will contain this information:

1. The author's name (last name first), followed by a period and one space.
2. The title, underlined and followed by a period and one space.
3. The city of publication, followed by a colon.
4. The shortened name of the publisher, followed by a comma.
5. The year of publication, followed by a period.

Notice that an entry has three main divisions separated from one another by a period and one space:

author   *title*   *publication*
(last name first)   *information*

Barsan, Richard Meran. <u>Non-Fiction Film</u>. New York:
Dutton, 1973.

Note: The 1995 MLA Handbook shows one space between main divisions but permits students to use two spaces if their instructor prefers this form.

The following examples illustrate some special situations in which you must vary this basic format.*

A book by one author

Zagorin, Perez. <u>The Court and the Country: The
    Beginning of the English Revolution</u>. New
    York: Atheneum, 1970.

When citing an edition other than the first, indicate the edition number in the form used on the work's title page.

Lawrence, William W. <u>Shakespeare's Problem
    Comedies</u>. 2nd ed. New York: Ungar, 1960.

If the book you are citing contains a title enclosed in quotation marks, keep the quotation marks. If the book contains an underlined title, however, do not underline it in your citation.

Herzog, Alan. <u>Twentieth Century Interpretations
    of "To a Skylark."</u> Englewood Cliffs:
    Prentice, 1975.

Knoll, Robert E., ed. <u>Storm Over The Waste Land</u>.
    Chicago: Scott, 1964.

A book by two or three authors

Only the first author's name is entered in reverse order; names of the second and third authors appear in normal order. Enter the

---

*MLA requires double-spacing within and between citations. Single-spacing has been used in the following examples to save space.

names in the order in which they appear on the title page. State each name in full even if two authors have the same last name.

```
Feldman, Burton, and Robert D. Richardson. The
     Rise of Modern Mythology. Bloomington:
     Indiana UP, 1972.
```

A book by more than three authors

For books with more than three authors, list only the first author followed by *et al.* (and others).

```
Prinz, Martin, et al. Guide to Rocks and
     Minerals. New York: Simon, 1978.
```

Two or more books by the same author

When listing two books by the same author, include the name in the first entry, but substitute three unspaced hyphens followed by a period in subsequent entries. Entries should be arranged alphabetically according to title.

```
Kingston, Maxine Hong. China Man. New York:
     Knopf, 1980.
---The Woman Warrior, New York: Vintage, 1977.
```

A multivolume work

If you use one volume of a multiple volume work, give the volume number and the total number of volumes, even if your paper refers to only one volume.

```
Brown, T. Allston. A History of the New York
     Stage. Vol. 2. New York: Blom, 1903. 2 vols.
```

A multivolume work in which each volume has an individual title

```
Durant, Will. The Renaissance. New York: Simon,
     1953. Vol. 5 of The Story of Civilization. 11
     vols. 1935-75.
```

An edited book

When listing an edited book, begin with the author if you refer mainly to the text itself.

> Melville, Herman. <u>Moby-Dick</u>. Ed. Charles
>   Fiedelson, Jr. Indianapolis: Bobbs, 1964.

If the citations in your paper refer to the work of the editor—the introduction, the editor's notes, or the editor's decisions in editing the text—put his or her name before the title.

> Fiedelson, Charles, Jr. ed. <u>Moby-Dick</u>. By Herman
>   Melville. Indianapolis: Bobbs, 1964.

An essay appearing in an anthology

When your paper refers to a single essay in a collection of essays, list the author of the essay first and include all the pages on which the full essay appears, even if you cite only one page in your paper.

> Forster, E. M. "Flat and Round Characters."
>   <u>Theory of the Novel</u>. Ed. Philip Stevick.
>   New York: Free,1980. 223-31.

If the essay you cite has been published previously, include publishing data for the first publication followed by the current information along with the abbreviation *Rpt. in* (Reprinted in).

> Ong, Walter J. "Literacy and Orality in our
>   Times." <u>ADE Bulletin</u> 58 (1978): 1-7. Rpt.
>   in <u>Composition and Literature: Bridging the
>   Gap</u>. Ed. Winifred Bryan Horner. Chicago: U of
>   Chicago P, 1983. 126-40.

A cross-reference

If you use more than one essay from a collection, list each essay separately, followed by a cross-reference to the entire collection. In addition, list complete publication information for the collection itself.

> Bolgar, R. R. "The Greek Legacy." Finley 429-72.

```
Davies, A. M. "Lyric and other Poetry." Finley
    93-119.
Finley, M. I., ed. The Legacy of Greece. New
    York: Oxford UP, 1981.
```

An introduction, preface, foreword, or afterword of a book

```
Beauvoir, Simone de. Preface. Treblinka. By
    Jean-Francois Steiner. New York: Mentor,
    1979. xiii-xxii.
```

A translation

```
Carpentier, Alejo. Reasons of State. Trans.
    Francis Partridge. New York: Norton, 1976.
```

An unsigned article in an encyclopedia

List an unsigned article the way it is cited in the encyclopedia. Because encyclopedia articles are arranged alphabetically, you may omit the volume and page numbers when citing one. You do not have to include publication information for well-known reference books.

```
"Liberty, Statue of." Encyclopaedia Britannica:
    Macropaedia. 1985.
```

A signed article in an encyclopedia

Cite a signed article by stating the author's last name first, followed by the article's title. When presenting reference books that are not very well known, present full publication information.

```
Grimstead, David. "Fuller, Margaret Sarah."
    Encyclopedia of American Biography. Ed. John
    A. Garraty. New York: Harper, 1974.
```

A reprint of an older edition

When citing a reprint of an older edition—a paperback edition of a hardback book, for example—give the original publication date and then the date of the reprint.

Greenberg, Daniel S. <u>The Politics of Pure
    Science</u>. 1967. New York: NAL, 1971.

A pamphlet

<u>Exisiting Light Photography</u>. Rochester: Kodak,
    1989.

A government publication

If no author is listed, treat the government agency as the author of
the publication. Give the name of the government followed by the
name of the agency. Underline the title and include the publishing
information that appears on the title page of the document.

United States. Dept. of State. <u>International
    Control of Atomic Energy: Growth of a Policy</u>.
    Washington: GPO, 1946.

A short story in an anthology

Faulkner, William. "A Rose for Emily." <u>To Read
    Literature</u>. Ed. Donald Hall. 2nd ed. New
    York: Holt, 1987. 4-10.

A short story in a collection

Stafford, Jean. "The Echo and the Nemesis."
    <u>The Collected Stories</u>. New York: Farrar,
    1970. 35-53.

A short poem in a collection

Enclose the title of a short poem in quotation marks.

Pound, Ezra. "A Virginal." <u>Selected Poems of Ezra
    Pound</u>. New York: New Directions, 1957. 23.

A book-length poem

Underline the title of a book-length poem.

> Eliot T. S. <u>The Waste Land</u>. <u>T. S. Eliot:</u>
> <u>Collected Poems 1909-1962</u>. New York:
> Harcourt, 1963. 51-70.

A play in an anthology

> Shakespeare, William. <u>Othello: The Moor of</u>
> <u>Venice. Shakespeare: Six Plays and the</u>
> <u>Sonnets</u>. Ed. Thomas Marc Parrott and Edward
> Hubler. New York: Scribner's, 1956.

Sample Citations: Articles

In general, a citation for a periodical article contains the following information:

1. The author's name (last name first) followed by a period and one space.*
2. The title of the article, enclosed within quotation marks, followed by a period and one space.*
3. The underlined title of the magazine or journal.
4. The volume number.
5. The date of publication, enclosed within parentheses, followed by a colon.
6. The inclusive pagination of the full article followed by a period.

However, when an article does not appear on consecutive pages—that is, it begins on page 30, skips to page 32, and ends on page 45—include only the first page of the article followed by a plus sign (30+ in this case).

The following examples illustrate variations on this format.

---

*You may use two spaces after the period if your instructor prefers.

An article in a scholarly journal with continuous pagination through an annual volume

A journal has continuous pagination if the pagination runs consecutively from one issue to the next throughout an annual volume (for example, one issue ends on page 252 and the next begins on page 253). In this case, you include the volume number of the journal in your citation.

```
LeGuin, Ursula K. "American Science Fiction and
    the Other." Science Fiction Studies 2 (1975):
    208-10.
```

An article in a scholarly journal with separate pagination in each issue

A citation for an article in a journal that begins with page 1 in each issue should include the volume number, a period, and then the issue number.

```
Farrell, Thomas J. "Developing Literate Writing."
    Basic Writing 2.1 (1978): 30-51.
```

An article in a weekly or biweekly magazine

To locate an article in a magazine, a reader needs a day, month, and year of publication, not the volume and issue numbers. In your citation, abbreviate all months except for May, June, and July.

```
Cuomo, Mario. "Family Style." New York 12 May
    1986: 84.
```

An unsigned article in a weekly or biweekly magazine

```
"Solzhenitsyn: An Artist Becomes an Exile."
    Time 25 Feb. 1974: 34+.
```

An article in a monthly or bimonthly magazine

In a citation for a magazine published monthly or bimonthly, give the month and year, not the volume and issue numbers.

```
Williamson, Ray. "Native Americans Were
     the First Astronomers." Smithsonian
     Oct. 1978: 78-85.
Gaspen, Phyllis. "Indisposed to Medicine: The
     Women's Self-Help Movement." The New
     Physicians May-June 1980: 20-24.
```

An article in a daily newspaper

Give the name of the newspaper as it appears on the first page of the paper, but omit the article (<u>Washington Post</u>, not <u>The Washington Post</u>). Give the date the article appeared, the edition, and the section if each section is numbered separately, and the page or pages on which the article appears.

```
Boffey, Phillip M. "Security and Science
     Collide on Data Flow." Wall Street Journal 24
     Jan. 1982, eastern ed.: 20.
"Madman Attacks Alligator." Smithville Observer
     14 Aug. 1981, late ed., sec. 4: 5+.
```

An editorial

```
Rips, Michael D. "Let's Junk the National
     Anthem." Editorial. New York Times
     5 July 1986, natl. ed.: A23.
```

A review

After a reviewer's name and the title of the review (if it has one), write *Rev. of* followed by the work that is reviewed, a comma, the word *by*, and the author. If the review has no listed author, begin with the title of the review. If the review has neither an author nor a title, begin with *Rev. of* and use the title of the work that is reviewed as a guide when you alphabetize the entry.

```
Nilsen, Don L. F. Rev. of American Tongue
     and Cheek: A Poplulist Guide to our
     Language, by Jim Quinn. College
     Composition and Communication 37
     (1986): 107-08.
```

A letter to the editor

```
Bishop, Jennifer. Letter. Philadelphia Inquirer.
    10 Dec. 1987: A26.
```

Sample Citations: Nonprint Sources

Material from a CD-ROM or other portable database

If the material you are citing appears not only in the portable database (CD-ROM, diskette, or magnetic tape) but also in a printed version, your citation should include the author of the material (if given); the title, source, and date of the printed version; the title of the database; the publication medium; the name of the vendor (if known); and the electronic publication date.

```
Russo, Michelle Cash. "Recovering from
    Bibliographic Instruction Blahs." RQ:
    Reference Quarterly 32 (1992) 178-83.
    Infotrac: Magazine Index Plus. CD-ROM.
    Information Access. Dec. 1993.
```

If the material you are citing appears in the database only and has no printed equivalent, include the author (if given); the title of the work; the title of the product; the publication medium; and publication information for the product (place, publisher, date).

```
Ellison, Ralph. Disklit: American Authors.
    Diskette. Boston: Hall, 1991.
```

Material from an on-line database

Enter material from an on-line database just as you would material from a portable database. Add the number of pages or paragraphs (if applicable), the name of the computer service or network, and the date of access.

```
Jansen, Lynn A. "Assessing Clinical Pragmatism."
    Kennedy Institute of Ethics Journal 8.1
    (1998): 3 Mar. 1998. 23-36. <http://Muse.jhu.
    edu/journals/kennedy_institute_of_ethics_
    journal/vOO8/8.1jansen.html>.
Accessed June 23, 1998.
```

Material available only on-line

Enter the title, author, date, and number of paragraphs.

```
Public Speech Statement of Senator Joe Lieberman
     in Support of the Conrad Television Ratings
     Amendment for June 13, 1995 [29 paragraphs]
     "TV Violence: Support of Conrad Amendment."
     3 June 1998.<http://www.senate.gov/member/ct
     /lieberman/ releases/support._conrad.html>
Accessed June 23, 1998.
```

A lecture

Give the name of the lecturer, the title, the location, and the date on which the lecture took place. Include the sponsoring organization if there is one, and supply a descriptive label if the lecture has no title.

```
Abel, Robert. "Communication Theory and Film."
     Communications Colloquium, Dept. of
     Humanities and Communications. Drexel U, 20
     Oct. 1986.
```

A personal interview

```
Fuller, Buckminster. Personal interview. 17 Dec.
     1980.
Davidowicz, Lucy. Telephone interview. 7 May
     1985.
```

A personal letter/e-mail

```
Walker, Alice. Letter to the author.
     8 June 1986.
Burke, James Lee. E-mail to the authors.
     15 Mar. 1995.
```

A film

Include the name of the film, the director, the distributor, the year, and any other information that you think is important. If you are emphasizing the contribution of any one person—the director, for example—begin with that person's name.

Lucas, George, dir. <u>Return of the Jedi</u>. Perf.
    Mark Hamill, Harrison Ford, Carrie Fisher,
    and Billy Dee Williams. Twentieth Century
    Fox, 1983.

A videocassette

<u>Arthur Miller: The Crucible</u>. Videocassette. Dir.
    William Schiff. Mosaic Group, 1987.

A television or radio program

Include the name of the program (underlined), the network, the
local station, the city, and the date of the program. You may also include other information that you think is important (the writers, for
example). If an individual program in a series has a title, include it
and put it in quotation marks.

<u>Nothing to Fear: The Legacy of F.D.R</u>. Narr. John
    Hart. NBC. KNBC, Los Angeles. 24 Jan. 1982.

"The Greening of the Forests." <u>Life on Earth</u>.
    Narr. David Attenborough. PBS. WHYY,
    Philadelphia. 26 Jan. 1982.

Content Notes

Content notes—multiple bibliographic citations or other material
that does not fit smoothly into the text—may be used along with
parenthetical documentation and are indicated by a raised number
in the text. The full text of these notes appears on the first full numbered page, entitled *Notes,* following the last page of the paper and
before the list of works cited.

For multiple citations

Use content notes for references to numerous citations in a single
reference. These references would be listed in the Works Cited section.

• In the paper

Just as the German and Russian Jews had
different religious practices, they also had
different experiences becoming Americanized.[1]

• In the note

>   ¹Glanz 37-38; Howe 72-77; Manners
> 50-52; and Glazer and Moynihan 89-93.

For explanations

Use notes to provide comments or explanations that are needed
to clarify a point in the text.

• In the paper

>   According to Robert Kimbrough, from the
> moment it was published, reviewers saw
> The Turn of the Screw as one of Henry
> James's most telling creations (169).[2]

• In the note

>   ²For typical early reactions to The Turn
> of the Screw, see Phelps 17; Woolf 65-67; and
> Pattee 206-07.

• In the paper

>   In recent years, Gothic novels have
> achieved great popularity.[3]

• In the note

>   ³Originally, Gothic novels were works
> written in imitation of medieval romances and
> relied on ghosts, supernatural occurrences, and
> terror. They flourished in the late eighteenth
> and early nineteenth centuries.

The Chicago Format

The Chicago Manual of Style* uses notes that appear at the bottom
of the page (footnotes) or at the end of the paper (endnotes)
and bibliographic citations at the end of the paper. Indent the first
line of each note and the second and subsequent lines of each
bibliographic citation three spaces. In both notes and bibliography,

---

*The Chicago format follows the guidelines set in *The Chicago Manual of Style.* 14th ed.
Chicago: University of Chicago Press, 1993.

single-space between the major divisions of each entry. The notes format uses a raised numeral at the end of the sentence in which you have either quoted or made reference to an idea or a piece of information from a source. This same number should appear at the beginning of the note. The first time you make reference to a work you use the full citation; *subsequent references* to the same work should list the author's last name, followed by a comma, and a page number. When more than one work by the same author is cited, a short title is necessary.*

- First note on Espinoza

      1. J. Manuel. Espinoza, <u>First Expedition
  of Vargas in New Mexico</u>, 1692 (Albuquerque:
  University of New Mexico Press, 1940), 10-15.

- Bibliographic form

  Espinoza, J. Manuel. <u>First Expedition of Vargas
      in New Mexico, 1692</u>. Albuquerque: University
      of New Mexico Press, 1940.

- Subsequent notes on Espinoza

  2. Espinoza, 69.
  3. Espinoza, 70.

If you are required to use *footnotes*, be sure that the note numbers on a particular page of your paper correspond to the footnotes at the bottom of the page. *Endnotes* are all of your notes on a separate sheet at the end of the paper under the title *Notes*.

Sample Citations for Notes: Books

A book by one author

      1. Herbert J. Gans, <u>The Urban Villagers</u>, 2d
  ed. (New York: Free Press, 1982), 100.

A book by two or three authors

      2.   James West Davidson and Mark Hamilton
  Lytle, <u>After the Fact: The Art of Historical
  Detection</u> (New York: Alfred Knopf, 1982), 54.

---

*The Chicago Manual of Style requires double-spacing within and between notes and bibliographic entries. Single-spacing has been used in the following examples to save space.

A multivolume work

> 3. Kathleen Raine, <u>Blake and Tradition</u> (Princeton: Princeton University Press, 1968), 1: 100.

> 4. Will Durant and Ariel Durant, <u>The Age of Napolean: A History of European Civilization From 1789 to 1815</u> vol. 11, <u>The Story of Civilization</u> (New York: Simon and Schuster, 1975), 90.

An edited book

> 5. William Bartram, <u>The Travels of William Bartram</u>, ed. Mark Van Doren (New York: Dover Press, 1955), 85.

An essay in an anthology

> 6. G.E.R. Lloyd, "Science and Mathematics," in <u>The Legacy of Greece</u>, ed. M.I. Finley (New York: Oxford University Press, 1981), 256-300.

An article in an encyclopedia (unsigned/signed)

> 7. <u>The Focal Encyclopedia of Photography</u>, 1965 ed., s.v. "Daguerreotype."

> 8. <u>The Focal Encyclopedia of Philosophy</u>, 1967 ed., s.v. "Hobbes, Thomas" by R. S. Peters.

The abbreviation *s.v.* stands for *sub verbo*—"under the word."

Sample Citations for Notes: Articles

An article in a scholarly journal with continuous pagination through an annual volume

> 1. John Huntington, "Science Fiction and the Future," <u>College English</u> 37 (fall 1975): 340-58.

An article in a scholarly journal with separate pagination in each issue

> 2. R. G. Sipes, "War, Sports, and Aggression: An Empirical Test of Two Rival Theories," American Anthropologist 4, no. 2 (1973): 84.

An article in a weekly magazine

> 3. Sharon Bergley, "Redefining Intelligence," Newsweek, 14 November 1983, 123.
>
> 4. "Solzhenitsyn: A Candle in the Wind," Time, 23 March 1970, 70.

An article in a monthly magazine

> 5. Lori Roll, "Careers in Engineering," Working Woman, November 1982, 62.

An article in a newspaper

> 6. Raymond Bonner, "A Guatemalan General's Rise to Power," New York Times, 21 July 1982, 3(A).

Sample Citations for Bibliographies: Books

A book by one author

> Gans, Herbert J. The Urban Villagers, 2d ed. New York: Free Press, 1982.

A book by two or more authors

> Davidson, James West, and Mark Hamilton Lytle. After the Fact: The Art of Historical Detection. New York: Alfred Knopf, 1982.

A multivolume work

> Raine, Kathleen. <u>Blake and Tradition</u>. Vol. 1.
>   Princeton: Princeton University Press, 1968.
> Durant, Will, and Ariel Durant. <u>The Age of
>   Napolean: A History of European Civilization
>   From 1789 to 1815</u> vol. 11, <u>The Story of
>   Civilization</u> New York: Simon and Schuster,
>   1975.

An edited book

> Bartram, William. <u>The Travels of William
>   Bartram</u>, edited by Mark Van Doren. New
>   York: Dover Press, 1955.

An essay in an anthology

> Lloyd, G.E.R. "Science and Mathematics."
>   <u>In The Legacy of Greece</u>, edited by M. I.
>   Finley, 256-300. New York: Oxford
>   University Press, 1981.

An article in an encyclopedia (unsigned/signed)

> <u>The Focal Encyclopedia of Photography</u> 1965 ed.,
>   s.v. "Daguerreotype."

> <u>The Focal Encyclopedia of Philosophy</u> 1967 ed.,
>   s.v. "Hobbes, Thomas," by R. S. Peters.

In a bibliography, these works are listed according to the name of the encyclopedia. Most encyclopedias are arranged alphabetically according to key terms. Providing the key word allows your reader to find the appropriate entry.

Sample Citations for Bibliographies: Articles

An article in a scholarly journal with continuous pagination through an annual volume

> Huntington, John. "Science Fiction and the
>   Future." <u>College English</u> 37 (fall 1975):
>   340-58.

An article in a scholarly journal with separate pagination in each issue

> Sipes, R. G. "War, Sports, and Aggression: An
>   Empirical Test of Two Rival Theories."
>   <u>American Anthropologist</u> 4, no. 2 (1973):
>   65-84.

An article in a weekly magazine

> Bergley, Sharon. "Redefining Intelligence."
>   <u>Newsweek</u>, 14 November 1983, 123.
> "Solzhenitsyn: A Candle in the Wind." <u>Time</u>, 23
>   March 1970, 70.

An article in a monthly magazine

> Roll, Lori. "Careers in Engineering." <u>Working
>   Woman</u>, November 1982, 62.

An article in a newspaper

> Bonner, Raymond. "A Guatemalan General's Rise to
>   Power." <u>New York Times</u>, 21 July 1982, 3(A).

Other Humanities Formats

Your instructor may require a format other than MLA or Chicago style. Most style manuals are readily available in the reference sections of libraries. *A Manual for Writers of Term Papers, Theses, and Dissertations* by Kate L. Turabian (The University of Chicago Press, 1973) is a style manual that uses formats based on the Chicago style.

Sample Student Papers in the Humanities

The following papers written by students in college classes illustrate the MLA, Chicago, and APA formats documentation. The progression of the development of each is traced in sidebars.

The religious studies paper "Beginning with the B's" compares and contrasts the rites of passage in the Jewish and Roman Catholic traditions. It is documented in MLA format.

The literature paper "*Rudolpho Anaga's Bless Me, Ultima: A Microcosmic Representation of Chicano Literature*" examines Anaga's first novel in the context of Mexican-American as well as universal experience. It is documented in MLA format.

The philosophy paper "Inner Vision" integrates experiences of the student with readings in philosophy and observations in painting and music. It has a title page and is documented in Chicago format.

The compositon research paper "The Dilemma of TV Violence" argues for government regulation of violence on television that is watched by small children. It was written in a composition class. However, since it deals with social science subject matter, it is documented in APA format, which is described in the chapter "Writing in the Social Sciences."

Sample Religious Studies Paper
Comparison/Contrast
with outline and sidebars
MLA Format

Julie Park
RS 150: Western Religious Traditions
Prof. Mary Joan Leith
November 7, 1997

Beginning with the B's

Thesis statement: One can analyze the Jewish *briss* and Roman Catholic baptism using two scholars' formulas to determine correlations between specific details of the ceremonies.

I. The *briss* is a rite of separation.
   A. First the male child is taken into the ceremonial room to separate him from his mother.
   B. Second the foreskin is cut to remove the barrier between the child and God.

II. Baptism is a rite of separation.
   A. First the child is brought into the church, a sacred place.
   B. The priest breathes on the child's face to separate the spirit of evil from the child.
   C. The priest places salt on the child's mouth.
   D. The priest lays his stole on the child as a sign from the church.

III. The *briss* is a rite of transition.
   A. The son leaves the room where his mother is confined.
   B. The son passes from the *kvatterin* to the *kvatter* and finally to the *sandek*.

IV. Baptism is a rite of transition.
   A. The priest introduces the child to the church.
   B. The sponsors make a profession of faith for the infant.
   C. The priest places spittle on the child's ears and nostrils.
   D. The priest anoints the child's breast and between his or her shoulders.

V.   The *briss* is the rite of incorporation
     for girls as well as for boys: Rituals
     symbolize the child's incorpaoration into
     the Jewish community.
  A. The child is embraced and accepted as a
     member of the Jewish community.
  B. The child is given a name.
  C. With the name, the child receives
     identity in the Jewish community.
VI. Baptism is a rite of incorporation:
    Rituals symbolize the child's
    incorporation into the Christian
    community.
  A. The child is cleansed with water.
  B. The priest makes the sign of the cross
     on the infant's forehead with water.
  C. The child receives its identity when
     the priest says its name.
  D. The child is anointed with chrism.
  E. The child receives a lighted candle.
 VII. Sacred time is present in *briss* and
      baptism.
   Judaism—Briss
   Christianity-Baptism

Park 1

Beginning with the B's
Julie Park

In the religious world there are many
different rites of passage which are
rituals performed at a turning point in a
person's life denoting a move from one
dimension in life to another. Every rite
of passage consists of different elements,
all important to the participants. These
elements are elaborated upon in the works of
Arnold van Gennep and Mircea Eliade. In
Arnold van Gennep's *Rites of Passage,* a rite
of passage is subdivided into three
components: rites of separation, transition
rites and rites of incorporation. Van Gennep
further states that "ceremonies for the
newborn child again involve a sequence of
rites of separation, transition and
incorporation" (Gennep 50). In addition to
the elements in Van Gennep's study, Mircea
Eliade and other writers describe other
characteristics such as the rite of passage
as the provider of a person's identity and
the source of sacred time. Eliade's set
of attributes corresponds largely to van
Gennep's elements. One can analyze the
Jewish *briss* and the Roman Catholic
baptism using the two scholars' ideas to
determine correlations between specific
details of the ceremonies.

  The *briss* ceremony can be broken down into
three parts, each part symbolizing the
elements set forth by Gennep. The first is
separation. According to Gennep "the child

*three components
of a rite of passage*

thesis

*introduction of rites
to be compared and
contrasted: briss and
baptism*

*discussion
of briss*

must first be separated from his previous environment . . ." (Gennep 50). Once the *briss* has begun the child has been separated twice: once from the womb and then from his mother when he is taken into the *briss* ceremonial room. The son must leave the surroundings he knows in order to receive his new life during circumcision. The son is also separated from the world of the dead. When he was born, he was given physical life, but he does not receive his spiritual life until the circumcision. The circumcision is the ritual that "frees him from the weight of dead Time, assures him that he is able to abolish the past, to begin his life anew, and to re-create his world . . ." (Eliade, *Myths* 139). Another aspect of separation is the actual cutting and removing of the foreskin. By removing the foreskin, the *mohel* is removing a barrier between the child and God, which impedes the Jewish from "perfecting the self in order to be closer to the Holy One" (Diamant I 10). Therefore, the child will later on be able to fully worship and love God. The son is now placed apart from the surrounding world and will be accepted into the Jewish faith. This acceptance finds its roots in the rites of transition and incorporation which constitute the remaining of the ceremony.

transition from first rite to second and third

Similar to the *briss*, the baptism has separation rites which allow the child (boy or girl) to leave his or her former life and start to make his or her way to a new spiritual life. At first the child is

comparison of baptism to briss

Park 3

separated from its former life by being
brought into the church, hence from profane
to sacred space. At the door the child who is
carried by his or her sponsors is met by the
priest who, after having the godparents ask
faith from the church of God in the child's
name, removes the evil spirit from the
child's face by breathing on it (Fanning
273). In comparison to the *briss* in which the
child is freed from dead Time, the baptism
purifies the child and severs his or her
bonds with the world of demonic figures. The
priest then places salt on the child's mouth.
During this act, the child "should be
delivered from the corruption of sin,
experience a relish of good works and be
delighted with the food of divine wisdom"
(273). The child successfully finishes the
separation phase when the priest lays his
stole on the child. With this sign from the
church, the child can smoothly move through
the remaining parts of the ceremony and
finish with a complete incorporation into the
church as well as the community.

The rites of transition for the newborn
Jewish son occur when he leaves the room
where his mother is confined. As he
passes through the doorway, he goes from
the world of the unliving where he had no
spiritual life to a place where upon being
incorporated he will lead a life of religious
devotion. Consequently, the son stands on the
threshold between the two worlds. The son also
experiences a rite of transition when he passes

picks up at second rite for Jewish son

from the *kvatterin* to the *kvatter* and finally
to the *sandek*. Every person that he
encounters contributes to his incorporation
into the Jewish spiritual world. The son must
pass through this transition phase because,
in order to go from one side to the other, a
threshold must be passed over. Once he has
crossed this threshold he can begin the rite
of incorporation.

transition to third rite

During the separation phase of the baptism,
the priest conducted all of the ablutions and
blessings at the doorway of the church or the
threshold between the sacred and the profane.
When the transition period of the ceremony
begins, the priest introduces the child to
the church and the sponsors make a profession
of faith for the infant while the priest, the
sponsors and the child move from the doorway
down the aisle of the church to the baptismal
font. When the priest places spittle on the
child's ears and nostrils, a correlation with
the Bible is set forth.

comparison of second phase of baptism to rite of transition in briss

> His nostrils and ears are next
> touched with spittle and he is im-
> mediately sent to the baptismal
> font, that, as sight was
> restored to the blind man men-
> tioned in the Gospel, whom the
> Lord, after having spread clay
> over his eyes, commanded to wash
> them in the waters of Siloe. . . .
> (273)

The child is also anointed on his or her
breast and between his or her shoulders with

the oils of the catechumen. After a
declaration of faith and call for baptism
aremade, the child has successfully gone
through the transition phase and is now
proceeding to the final incorporation
elements (273).

   The final part of the *briss* ceremony
involves rites of incorporation. Once the
mohel has circumcised and drawn blood from
the penis, the Jewish faith embraces the
child and accepts him as one of its members.

return to briss *for discussion of third rite: incorporation*

Although the daughters cannot have a
circumcision, they still have an official
ceremony welcoming them into the Jewish
faith. The daughter's ceremony corresponds to
the final part of the son's ritual once he
has been circumcised. They are both given
their names and blessings at this point.
Whereas the son is usually given his name at
home during the *briss,* the daughter has her
name announced in the synagogue during her
father's Torah service. Now that the child
has a name, he or she has an identity in the
Jewish faith. Gennep says, "when a child is
named, he is both individualized and
incorporated into society" (62). This
identity is sealed when the *mohel* and father
bless the son or daughter asking God to watch
over them and give them guidance.

> When a child is born, he has only a
> physical existence; he is not yet
> recognized by his family nor ac-
> cepted by the community . . . it is
> only by virtue of those rites that

he is incorporated into the community of the living. (Eliade, *Sacred*
184-185)

The child now has a new status in the world.
He can begin to make a life for himself
within the confines of the Jewish faith.

During the last stage of the baptism,
the incorporation, the main purpose of the
baptism occurs: the baby is cleansed with
water and signed with the cross. The priest
makes the sign of the cross on the infant's
forehead with water while saying ". . . N . . .
I baptize thee in the name of the Father and
the Son and the Holy Ghost" (Fanning 273).
Corresponding to the removal of the foreskin
and the symbolic barrier in the *briss,* the
ritual of cleansing and signing with the
water erases the hindrance between the child
and God; "this washing is not a mere
purification rite but the sacrament of being
joined to Christ" (Mitchell 127). Once the
priest has said the child's name while
administering the three-fold ablution, the
child receives its identity. The child will
now be able to worship God and study the
Bible and Catechism just as the Jewish child
studies the Torah. Next the child is anointed
again with chrism "to give him to understand
that from the day he is united as a member to
Christ, his head, and engrafted on His body;
and therefore he is called a Christian from
Christ but Christ from chrism" (Fanning 273).

*comparison
of third rite
of baptism
to rite of
incorpora-
tion in* briss

Park 7

The child is now a member of the Christian
faith. At this time a white veil is placed
over him or her and he or she receives a
lighted candle. The ceremony is completed
when the new Christian is bidden to go in
peace (273). The community now has a new
member through which the spirit of Jesus and
the community will live and prosper.

Within the context of the *briss* and the
baptism, the community is involved. Even
though the *briss* is held within the home and
the baptism is sometimes held in the church
with only the family members present, the
community still learns lessons because with
each baptism the same lessons are learned.
The *briss* ritual in every part has teachings
for every Jewish person. The blessings for
example remind them of their devotion and of
the life they should lead. For every newborn
son that is circumcised, God's promise to
Abraham is repeated. With this revelation the
Jews are protected. Every circumcision
safeguards their community because once a
child is accepted into the community, he or
she "will safeguard spiritual survival . . ."
(Trepp 216). The Jewish people trust the
youth just as Abraham trusted God. The Roman
Catholic community learns about the Lord's
death and resurrection when baptism is
conducted. "On Sunday, baptism may be
celebrated even during Mass, so that the
entire community may be present and the
necessary relationship between baptism and
eucharist may be clearly seen . . ."
(Mitchell 12). The community strengthens its
bond with every child that is baptized.

*discussion of
common
elements in*
briss *and*
baptism

importance of briss *and* baptism

Whether it is the Jewish *briss* or the Roman Catholic baptism, the ceremony provides the child with an identity not only in the church but in the community as well. For Judaism circumcision is a symbol of a covenantal commitment between God and Abraham. "You shall circumcise the flesh of your foreskins and it shall be a sign of the covenant between me and you" (Oxford, 2 1). Since the history of Abraham is so important to the Jewish people, practicing circumcision reinforces in them their Jewish identity. According to Theodore Gaster (*The Holy and the Profane,* p. 53), "the covenantal commitment is the raison d'etre of the Jewish faith." Therefore by "making" *brisses* and circumcising sons, Jews reaffirm their selfhood within their religion. In Roman Catholicism, baptism is an important part of the faith because the child is then accepted as a member and allowed to receive communion.

Through the sacraments of Christian initiation, we are freed from the power of darkness and joined to Christ's death, burial, and resurrection. We receive the Spirit of filial adoption and are part of the entire people of God, in the celebration of the memorial of the Lord's death and resurrection (Mitchell, 125-126).

With the separation, transition and incorporation of themes within the rites of passage, the child receives this identity and lessons as well. With the "completion of the conversion of Christ's claims, the unification with the community founded by Christ and the forgiveness of sins" (Sherman 134), the child can live a healthy, happy life under the guidance of the community.

Eliade states that "by means of rites religious man can pass without danger from the ordinary temporal duration to sacred time" (Eliade, *Sacred,* 68). Therefore, this sacred time is exemplified in the rituals of the *briss* and the baptism. In sacred time one relives the time when God was at work. In Judaism, when the Jews "make" a *briss* they are reliving the time when God made the covenant with Abraham. They are present with God every time they witness a circumcision. "Rituals periodically reconfirm the sacredness of their origins and re-establish 'sacred' time for the community performing the rituals" (Eliade, *Myths* 133). With the new Jewish member of the culture, the Jews witness a new world. The birth of the newborn indicates the birth of a new world for the Jewish people. The briss constitutes a sacred time because it does not matter where the ceremony takes place but when it takes place. The time at which the newborn is inducted into the Jewish faith is holy. The *briss* occurs on the eighth day so that the child can experience its first Sabbath and because

both rites establish sacred time

it was believed that the parents have not yet
forgotten the miracle of birth.

For Christianity the baptism exhibits
certain aspects of sacred time with respect
to when it is usually held. It is
"recommended that the sacrament be celebrated
during the Easter Vigil or on Sunday when the
Church commemorates the Lord's resurrection"
(Mitchell 11-12). The events that surrounded
Jesus' life are extremely important to
Christians. Therefore, when bringing a new
Christian into the faith, Jesus' death and
resurrection are introduced as the beginning
of the Christian's spiritual life. In
addition the different aspects of the baptism
repeat various occurrences from Biblical
times. Jesus' baptism is kept in the
foreground of the minds of the people
participating in the baptism.

> The three central liturgical actions
> of the sacrament—the washing, the
> anointing, and the laying of hands
> (when the priest blessed the child)—
> were identified with the events in
> the baptism of Jesus: the baptism by
> John, the descent of the Holy Spirit
> "like a dove," and the voice of the
> Father proclaiming his Sonship. (5)

The sponsors, who are either holding the baby
or touching it, make professions of faith for
the child so that he or she will grow through
the teachings of Jesus (Fanning 273). The
Christians not only are remembering the

baptism of Jesus but also his resurrection. These teachings are so vital to the proper spiritual growth of the child that the necessary declarations of faith are proclaimed and the child is baptized as a future member of Christ's kingdom.

Both the Jewish and Roman Catholic birth rites are the starting of spiritual life. They entail many rituals that all constitute many aspects of the Jewish and Roman Catholic culture. Being Protestant and having the same basic practices as the Roman Catholic Church, I knew the major parts involved in the baptism. Yet I lacked knowledge of the Jewish birth ceremony. Upon learning about the different Jewish rituals, I have learned about how strong the Jewish faith is and how important it is to the Jews. With the correlations that I made between the Jewish and Roman Catholic birth rituals, I now have a deeper sense of the baptism and a clear understanding of the Jewish faith. The *briss* and the baptism are truly monumental occasions that stir many emotions in the community and now in myself.

Works Cited

Asheri, Michael. *Living Jewish*. 2nd ed. New York: Everett House, 1978.

Diamant, Anita. *The Jewish Baby Book*. New York: Summit, 1988.

Eliade, Mircea. *Myths, Rites, Symbols*. Ed. Wendell C. Beane and William G. Doty. New York: Harper & Row, 1975.

- - -. *The Sacred and the Profane*. San Diego: Harcourt, 1987.

Fanning, William H.W. "Baptism." *The Catholic Encyclopedia*. 1913 ed.

Gaster, Theodore. *The Holy and the Profane, Evolution of Jewish Folkways*. New York: William Morrow, 1955.

Gennep, Arnold van. *Rites of Passage*. 1960. New York: University of Chicago Press, 1973.

Metzer, Bruce M. *The New Oxford Annotated Bible*. New York: Oxford UP, 1994.

Mitchell, Leonel L. *Worship: Initiation and the Churches*. Washington, D.C.: Pastoral Press, 1991.

Sherman, Anthony. "Baptism." *Encyclopedia of Catholicism*. 1995 ed.

Trepp, Leo. *A History of the Jewish Experience: Eternal Faith, Eternal People*. New York: Behrman House, 1962.

Sample Literature Paper
with title page and side bars
MLA Format

Rudolfo Anaya's <u>Bless Me, Ultima</u>:
A Microcosmic Representation of Chicano
Literature

by

Jennifer Flemming

English 3112

Dr. Jussawalla

May 12, 1998

Flemming 1

Underline title of published work.

Rudolfo Anaya's <u>Bless Me, Ultima</u>:
A Microcosmic Representation of Chicano
Literature

Chicano authors have sometimes been called
"noble savages" and they have been denied
credit and recognition in the field of
literature and culture. Some scholars and
teachers consider Chicano literature as
"newly emerged" from recent political
developments and therefore lacking in
maturity and universal appeal, although
others have traced its growth and development
in the Southwest since the sixteenth century.
The fact that most Chicano literature is
based on social protest and is associated
with political events also elicits less than
positive responses from literary critics. The
political nature of the literature causes it
to be viewed as not quite legitimate.
However, Chicano literature is neither "newly
emerged" and thus lacking in maturity, nor
merely reflective of recent socio-political
movements. On the contrary, Chicano
literature—writing done by American
Hispanics—not only records the
Mexican-American experience in the American
Southwest but also demonstrates the

thesis universality of experience. <u>Bless Me, Ultima</u>,
the first novel of Rudolpho Alfonso Anaya
(born in Pastura, New Mexico, on October 30,
1927) records the Mexican-American experience
while describing the emotions universal to
most ten-year-old boys, thus exemplifing the
dual role of the best Chicano literature.

Flemming 2

Paredes and Paredes's definition of Chicano literature ties it to the Chicano's key role in the cultural development of the American Southwest:

> People like to record their experiences; Mexican-Americans have been no exception. They have had much to write about. Their lives have sometimes been stormy and often tragic, but always vital and intriguing. It is hardly surprising that Mexican-Americans have literary talents, for they are heirs to the European civilization of Spain and the Indian civilizations of Mexico, both of which produced great poets and storytellers. Furthermore, they have also been in contact with the history and literature of the United States . . . . (1)

Indent a quote of four lines or more.

Put page number in parentheses outside period at the end of an indented long quote if the author's name and the title of the work are given in the text.

This connection of the development of the literature with the locale is made by Luis Leal in his article "Mexican American Literature: A Historical Perspective," when he notes that Chicano literature had its origin when the Southwest was settled by the inhabitants of Mexico during colonial times (22). He emphasizes that the literature originated both from the contact of the colonial Mexicans with the Native Americans and from the contact with the Anglo culture that was moving westward. In fact, many of the themes of Chicano literature emphasize the coming in contact of two vastly different

Put a parenthetical citation inside period at end of paraphrased information if the name of the author and the title of the work are given in the text.

cultures. This is particularly true of Anaya'a *Bless Me, Ultima,* which also reflects the universal emotions and feelings generated as a result of the clash of cultures.

A recording of the experience of the Southwest is found in Anaya's *Bless Me, Ultima*, which also relates universal themes of initiation and maturation (Novoa, "Themes"). In his novel about the rites of passage of a young boy (Antonio) from innocent adolescence to the ambiguous and morally corrupt adult world, the author expresses his culture's indigenous beliefs, myths, and legends.

Antonio's father tells him of the coming of the Spanish colonizers to the Valley, their contact with the American-Indian culture which Ultima—an older grandmother figure—exemplifies, and the changes brought about in the village and the town by the coming of the *Tejanos* . Yet the theme is universal, transcending the boundaries of his village. The events that result from the clash between the old and the new could take place anywhere in the world because they deal with religious hatred and with the conflicts between different ways of life.

The novel relates the story of a young boy and his friendship with a *curandera* (shaman) named Ultima who comes to live with Antonio and his family. The arrival of Ultima has an enormous impact on him because he feels a kinship with her. For instance, through Ultima, Antonio—now nicknamed Tony—comes in contact with the local Indian religions.

Ultima teaches him about herbs and their potency in creating conditions often associated with magic. She also introduces Antonio to Narcisso, the Indian who teaches him the myth of the Golden Carp: "The people who killed the carp of the river . . . were punished by being turned into fish themselves. After that happened many years later, a new people came to live in this valley" (Anaya 110). This myth encapsulates the history of the Indian people, the Hispanic colonizers, and the Anglo settlers of New Mexico. Tony sees the reflection of the myth in his day-to-day life. The Indians and the Hispanics of the valley are an gradually replaced by the "new people," the Anglos. This stirs in him deep love for his land, his people, and his lifestyle.

Put last name of author and page number in parenthesis if title of work is already given.

But at school he is teased for believing in these myths. His classmates, who have already laughed at his lunch of tortillas and his inability to speak English, taunt him about Ultima. Calling her a <u>bruja</u> (witch) they say, "Hey, Tony, can you make the ball disappear?" "Hey, Tony, do some magic" (Anaya 102). Tony suffers the angst of a ten-year-old taunted by these voices. He begins to suffer doubts about his identity and the rightness of his beliefs.

At the end of the book, when Ultima is killed by the townspeople for being a witch, Antonio falls to his knees to pray for her and in facing her death reaches his maturation. He knows what is right for him:

"I praised the beauty of the Golden Carp" (Anaya 244).

Anaya has said, "When people ask me where my roots are, I look down at my feet. . . . They are here, in New Mexico, in the Southwest" (Novoa, Chicano Authors 185). The author's message is clear and undeniable: One must know one's roots, despite the conflicting pull of Americanization. It is the same message of faith and hope that Ultima, on her deathbed, gives to Antonio: learn to accept life's experiences and feel the strength of who you are. In the character of Ultima, however, Anaya has created a symbol of beauty, harmony, understanding, and the power of goodness that transcends the limits of time and space and religious beliefs.

Bless Me, Ultima was written in 1972. Anaya's subsequent novels continue his interpretation of the lives of Hispanics living in the southwestern United States. His second novel, Heart of Axtlan (1976) concentrates on the urban experience of the Chicano; Tertuga (1979) examines the spiritual experiences of Chicanos. Albuquerque (1992) is the story of a Chicano boxer's search for his father. (Latino Literature Web Page). These are universal concerns as well as elements of Mexican-American life. Anaya's work records the Mexican-American experience of the Southwest while creating characters and portraying emotions of universal appeal. The social

Put last name of author, title of work, and page number in parentheses at end of in-text quote.

protest against Americanization is secondary
to the treatment of myth and emotions.

Chicano literature cannot be considered
just a byproduct of the struggle for civil
rights. This is not to minimize or deny the
effects of the Chicano political movement and
the sense of awareness and direction it has
sparked (which includes the proliferation of
Chicano literary texts). Although Chicano
literature may appear to emphasize social
protest and criticism of the dominant Anglo
culture, or seem to be introspectively
searching for self-definition, it will not
be found lacking in universal appeal
(Leal et al. 42).

Works Cited

Anaya, Rudolfo. Bless Me, Ultima. Berkeley:
Tonatiuh, 1972.

Anaya, Rudolpho. Latino Literature Web Page.
<http://www.ollusa.edu/alumni/alumni/latino/
anaya.htm>. 1 May 1998.

Jimenez Francisco. The Indentification and
Analysis of Chicano Literature. New York:
Bilingual, 1979.

Leal, Luis, et al. A Decade of Chicano
Literature. Santa Barbara: La Causa, 1982.

- - -. "Mexican American Literature: A
Historical Perspective." Modern Chicano
Writers. Eds. Joseph Sommera and Tomas
Ybarra-Fausto. Englewood Cliffs: Prentice,
1979. 18-40.

Martinez, Julio A., and Franciaco A. Lomeli.
Chicano Literature: A Reference Guide.
Westport: Greenwood, 1985.

Novoa, Juan-Bruce. "Themes in Rudolfo Anaya's
Work." Talk given at New Mexico State
University. Las Cruces, 11 Apr. 1987.

- - -. Chicano Authors: Inquiry by Interview.
Austin: U of Texas P, 1980.

Paredes, Americo, and Raymond Paredes.
Mexican-American Authors. Boston: Houghton,
1973.

Sample Philosophy Paper
with title page and side bars
Chicago Format

Inner Vision

Nancy Freitas
Department of Philosophy
November 1996

Inner Vision

quote from artist

Well, what shall I say; our inward thoughts, do they ever show out-wardly? There may be a great fire in our soul, but no one ever comes to warm himself at it, and the passers-by see only a bit of smoke coming through the chimney, and pass on their way.

van Gogh, Letter of July 1880, 122

introductory reflection

A new born day awaits us. A beautiful sunny, warm summer day brightens me. I enjoy the peace and tranquillity of Stonehill's landscape. It is the first day of my college experience. I feel worried and very much excited. I keep asking myself, what will become of my experiences in this new environment? I begin to wonder what my philosophy class is all about. It is 11:15 and I make my way to class.

assignment to see, hear, and seek

In class our professor tells us to write about what philosophy means to us as students. We must note the things we see, hear, or seek in our walk, in certain illustrations, in some music, and in our readings of a letter from July of 1880 by van Gogh and "The Apology" by Plato. Though at first the reason for these activities was vague, slowly I began to see that each can be seen as a draft, a sketch, a sentence of my life. Little by little, these activities formed a harmonious whole, a picture, a musical composition, a narrative of who I am.

Freitas 2

How true and how beautiful for me now is the parallel that van Gogh makes between life and painting when he writes to his brother Theo these words:

relates reflection to quote by van Gogh

> What is your definite aim? That aim becomes more definite, will stand out slowly and surely, just as the rough draft becomes a sketch, and the sketch becomes a picture, little by little, by working seriously on it, by pondering over the idea, vague at first, over the thought that was fleeting and passing, till it gets fixed (van Gogh, p. 120).

It is this process, this construction of my fleeting and passing moments into a living present, into a fixed idea, into an inner vision that I wish to sketch in this paper.

As I begin my sketch, I see the dew drops settle in the late summer grass. A small hill leads me to a statue of Jesus. He stares down at me from the cross; and, as I recall the pain that he went through for mankind, a tear falls from my eye. I wonder how my own life is connected to Jesus. For a while, I am spellbound, almost immobile. As I look up at Jesus from a bench, a memory of the day when my great aunt died comes to mind. The pain and sorrow that my family felt on that cold November day return, as though I am once again reliving her death. I remember a quote from Socrates that makes me realize my beloved aunt has just gone to live in another place: "Let us reflect ... we shall see that

images perceived by eyes, expressed in writing

visual perception and readings related to memories

... death is a good ... is a change and migration of the soul from this world to another place" (Plato, p. 422). I am also reminded of the text in the New Testament which tells us of Jesus' resurrection. Like Jesus, I believe that my aunt's body will be resurrected to live eternally in Heaven. I take one last look at Jesus, and then I walk to a nearby wall. I look over and see a stream moving rather slowly. It seems as though the water is asleep, not yet awakened by the sun's gleaming rays of light. As I

integration of visual and mental images

turn my head, I see that the wind slowly makes the trees dance. I leave the sleeping stream and move under the shade of a lively tree. A grasshopper sits and seems to stare at me. Never before have I focused so sharply on a bug. The grasshopper jumps all around, but never leaves my sight. Nothing takes away the amazement. Wonder and joy control every part of me. I am in total rapture just looking at this insect. I could stay forever looking at this grasshopper. The walk then takes me to a rock formation whose perfection absorbs me. It is all natural, not man made. I feel as though this rock is speaking to me,

integration of auditory images and memories

telling me to see or read its life, its origin. As this walk comes to an end, I begin to understand Lucretius' philosophy: we are just mirrors of nature.

I hurry back to meet the group. We sit near a tall, newly built building and listen to some music. The music begins. It is so happy and free. Suddenly I am taken back to my first carnival, recalling how amazed I was at the height of the ferris wheel. I even remember the clouds on that day, so puffy in the clear blue sky, somewhat like the sky of today. I grasp this memory, I have it in my mind, I hold on to it, as though I am reliving it now. And, as I hear the quiet sound of flutes and clarinets, I soar slowly above the material world into the intelligible world, the world of memory, of my inner eye. What I see now is not only the rock, the grasshopper, the running water, the statue of Jesus that I saw earlier, but also images of misfortune, of my aunt's death, of my change from youth to adulthood. As the music fades and becomes quieter, I begin to hear my mother singing to me, recalling the time she put me to sleep. At this moment, her song and the music join together into a peaceful sound which puts me to sleep. The music becomes even more dear to me as I go from just seeing and hearing to embracing myself in my memories.

Similarly, the illustrations we saw also allow me to dwell in the world of my memories. As my memories come to life in my mind, I feel myself leaving the cave that Plato wrote about. Mentally, I escape into a new-found world of knowledge. As I look at picture three, the little girl that is so involved with her cake makes me remember my eighth birthday. I can see again my special Mickey Mouse cake, as my friends and family surrounded me, waiting for me to make a wish, and to blow out those eight candles plus one for good luck. The memories of my deceased

integration of visual and mental images

great aunt return once again as I look at picture seven, a scene of death. I can hear her voice so clearly; it will always linger in my mind. She still seems so close to me, and I miss her now even more. That same scene also brings me to the girl in picture one, who is in a state of reflection, of wondering about life, as though she says with Socrates that "the unexamined life is not worth living" (Plato, p. 420). Feelings of sorrow, of loneliness, of anguish, of doubt—all coincide in picture two, where we see a man in a moment of loss. The way I freed myself from these feelings is also revealed to me in illustrations numbers three, four, five, eight, and nine—all of which deal with love and joy. Happiness is no longer hidden in the darkness that I once thought was my destiny. Maybe this is just one of the many phases that everyone has to experience, as in picture six, the life cycle. To see my own life cycle in these illustrations is indeed to say with van Gogh: "*How rich art is, if one can only remember what one has seen, one is never empty of thoughts or truly lonely, never alone*" (van Gogh, p. 116).

use of quote to bring visual, auditory, and mental images together

Our first class has come to an end. My memories have been awakened during this past hour by seeing, hearing, and reading, as van Gogh would say, my own life as I recall it, as I bring it to consciousness in my mind. As for my philosophy class, I now realize that the activities we did were a way to reach personal perfection, to see existence with an inner eye. Now, it is clear to me that

thesis

philosophy is becoming aware of oneself, of
loving oneself, of freeing oneself from the
prejudices, the ignorance, the constraints of
the material world. Or, as van Gogh stated
it: "Do you know what frees one from this
captivity? [I]t is very deep serious
affection. Being friends, being brothers,
love, that is what opens the prison by
supreme power, by some magic force" (van
Gogh, p. 126). I am becoming inwardly free.

*use of quote
to conclude*

Bibliography

Gogh, Vincent van. *The Letters of Vincent van Gogh*. Edited by Mark Roskill. New York: Atheneum, 1972.

Plato. "The Apology." Vol. I of *The Dialogues of Plato*. Translated by B. Jowett. New York: Random House, 1937.

Sample Composition Research Paper
with side bars and Web sites
APA Format

Paper #6: Argument   Kevin Fitzgibbon
College Composition   April 18, 1996

The Dilemma of TV Violence

Every Saturday morning, kids all over America get up early and turn on the television to watch their "toons." Some of these cartoons display violent interaction between characters for the mere purpose of making children laugh. But does the violent content in some cartoons affect children adversely and should these cartoons therefore be censored? Personally I believe that kids should not be allowed to watch certain violent cartoons because of the potential negative effects.   *thesis*

   The UCLA Television Violence Monitoring Report by the UCLA Center for Communication Policy surveyed Saturday morning cartoons that would raise concern in most viewers. They found that only 23% of the cartoons raised concern in viewers; however, those 23% of cartoons were the most viewed including the popular Mighty Morphins, Power Rangers and X-MEN. These shows were classified as "Sinister Combat Violence," because the shows "are obsessed primarily with violence, the whole story line leads to violence, and the main characters are always pre-occupied with using violence to get their ways."   *evidence from research*

   The American Academy of Child and Adolescent Psychiatry found that children can average up to three to four hours of watching television a day and believe that "television can be a powerful influence in developing value system and shaping behavior." After hundreds of studies of kids who watch that   *evidence from research*

much violent television, including "Sinister
Combat Violence," they found that children
will "become 'immune' to the horror of
violence, gradually accept it as a way to
solve problems, and imitate the violence they
observe on television." They found children
who watch television extensively will become
more aggressive; however, the "impact may . . .
surface years later and young people can even
be affected when the family atmosphere shows
no tendency towards violence."

recognition and refutation of an opposing argument

There are those who say that if a child is
vulnerable to violence in cartoons, then
children will be affected just as badly by
the violence in books and media sources.
However books, television news and newspapers
are a medium to violence that does not
interest kids as much as a simple cartoon.
Children's interest in cartoons comes at an
age when they are very impressionable; and,
although children will grow to be interested
in other sources of information containing
violence, they will be mature enough not to
be adversely influenced.

argument to support position

Due to the possible negative effects of
cartoons, television programs should be
regulated just like anything that is
potentially dangerous to our health or
development. Just as drugs are regulated to
protect the physical well-being of American
citizens, cartoon violence should be
regulated to protect the mental development
of children. As Senator Joe Lieberman says in
his speech supporting the Conrad Television
Ratings Amendment:

TV Violence 2

But we must also remember that we are leaders as well as lawmakers. That is why I want to commend my colleague, Senator Conrad, for forcing this body to weigh carefully the ramifications of this legislation for America's families, and for our moral health. Why is this so important now? Because at the very moment that new technologies are exploding through the roof, the standards of television programs are plunging through the floor, with the velocity of a safe dropping off a cliff in a vintage Road Runner cartoon. Except, instead of Wile E. Coyote, it is the values and sensibilities of our children that are put in peril.

Because of the First Amendment, there are those who believe it is wrong to regulate television programs The First Amendment was intended to protect media sources' rights to expose truth to the people and was not meant to protect television programs which distort children's idea of reality and confuse children about the concept of violence. With the Constitution's flexibility, the government should exercise more control as the computer age arises and more sources of violence can be found. However, censorship responsibilities should not fall just on the television programs; parents should be the primary regulators of what their children

recognition and refutation of an opposing argument

TV Violence 3

watch on television. But when parents' backs
are turned, children's choice should be
limited to nonviolent programs or programs
that have a controlled amount of violence
which is only humorous.

The findings of hundreds of experiments are
conclusive: violence on television affects
children's behavior adversely. With this kind
of evidence, the government should be
obligated to regulate the television industry
just as it does any other industry which
produces dangerous products; however, this
censorship should not infringe on the
intended rights of the First Amendment.

conclusion

References

The American Academy of Child and Adolescent
Psychiatry. "Children & TV Violence" 6 May
1996. Available Internet: http://www.psych.
med.umich.edu/web/aacap/factsfam/violence.htm

Mediascope Inc. "Two New Studies on
Television Violence and Their Significance
for the Kid's TV Debate" Available Internet:
http://www.cep.org/tvviolence html

Public speech Statement of Senator Joe
Lieberman in Support of the Conrad Television
Ratings Amendment for June 13, 1995 [29
paragraphs] "TV Violence: Support of Conrad
Amendment." Available Internet: http://www.
senate.gov/member/ct/ lieberman/releases/
support_conrad html

*references w
Web addres
in APA styl*

Reprinted with permission from *Prologue*. Easton,
Massachusetts: Stonehill College, 1997.

WRITING IN THE
SOCIAL SCIENCES

The social sciences include the following subject areas: anthropology, criminal justice, economics, education, political science, psychology, social work, and sociology. Writing in the social sciences differs from writing in the humanities in that its format conforms to the particular objective of the project or research: exploration, description, explanation, or evaluation. Descriptive and explanatory formats are the dominant forms for the presentation of information in psychology, sociology, anthropology, and political science, where they not only describe individual patterns but also provide explanations of the dynamics of a group, such as a political organization.

Research Sources

Library research is an important component of research in the social sciences. Only after the researcher has developed a sufficient foundation for the study through library research can he or she pursue data collection through interviews, questionnaires, and field observations. Social scientists survey attitudes, record responses, and interview subjects to obtain reliable evidence. Many of their data are numerical, reported in tables and charts. It is essential for social scientists to know how to read and interpret such figures so that they can analyze data and develop conclusions. Much of your library research in social science disciplines will depend on abstracting information from such tables and charts. Therefore, general reference sources like government yearbooks and almanacs may be particularly useful.

Specialized Library Sources

The following reference sources are useful in a variety of social science disciplines.

ASI Index (American Statistics Index)
International Bibliography of the Social Sciences
International Encyclopedia of the Social Sciences
PAIS Public Affairs Information Service
Social Sciences Citation Index
Social Science Abstracts

The following reference sources are most often used for research in specific disciplines.

Anthropology

Abstracts in Anthropology
Anthropological Index

Business and Economics

Business Periodicals Index
Economic Literature Index

Criminal Justice

Abstracts on Criminology and Penology
Abstracts on Police Science
Criminal Justice Abstracts
Criminal Justice Periodicals Index

Education

ERIC
Education Index

Political Science

ABC Political Science
CIS Index (Congressional Information Service)
United States Political Science Documents

Psychology

*Author Index to Psychological Index and Psychological
    Abstracts Cumulative Subject
Index to Psychological Abstracts
Psychological Abstracts*

Sociology

*Sage Family Studies Abstracts
Sociological Abstracts*

Government Documents

Government documents are important resources for social
scientists. They contain the most complete and up-to-date facts and
figures necessary for any social analysis. Varied information—
from technical, scientific, and medical information to everyday
information on home safety for children—can be found in
government documents.

Government documents can be searched through the *Monthly
Catalog,* which contains the list of documents published that month
together with a subject index. Other indexes include The
*Congressional Information Service Index, The American Statistics
Index* and *The Index to U.S. Government Periodicals.* The U.S.
government now maintains many Web sites.

Newspaper Articles

Newspaper articles are particularly useful sources for researching
subjects in political science, history, economics, or social work.
Students usually rely on the *New York Times,* which has indexes
available both in print and on microfilm. However, for newspaper
information from across the country, a handy and useful source
is *Newsbank. Newsbank,* like the government's *Monthly Catalog,*
provides subject headings under the appropriate government
agencies. For instance, articles on child abuse are likely to be listed
under Health and Human Services. Older articles will be listed in
older *Newsbanks* under Health, Education, and Welfare. Once you
find the subject area, *Newsbank* provides a microcard/microfiche
number. On that microfiche, you will find articles from around the
country on your subject.

Specialized Databases for Computer Searches

Many of the print sources cited above have electronic counterparts. Some of the more widely used databases for social science disciplines include *Cendata, Business Periodicals Index, PsycINFO, ERIC, Social Scisearch, Sociological Abstracts, Information Science Abstracts, PAIS International, Population Bibliography, Education Literature Index, BI/INFORM, Legal Resources Index, Management Contents, Trade and Industry Index, and PTS F+S Indexes.*

The World Wide Web (www) offers a wealth of information; however, since anyone can put anything on the Web, students must be careful to check the credibility of the authors of Web site information.

The following Web sites should lead to reliable sources. Notice that these are maintained and updated by universities and organizations that control the quality of the information that they list. The individual sites are subject to change.

Anthropology:
<http://www.sscf.ucsb.edu/anth/netinfo.html>
< http://humanitas.ucsb.edu:80/shuttle/anthro.html>

Economics:
<http://www.bschool.ukans.edu/intbuslib/virtual.htm>

International Law:
<http://www.law.ecel.uwa.edu.au/intlaw/>

Political Science:
<http://www.agora.stm.it/politic/>
<http://www.pitt.edu/-ian/ianres.html>

Psychology:
<http://www.wesleyan.edu/spn>
<http://www.psych-web.com/resource/bytopic.htm>

Sociology:
<http://www.pscw.uva.nl/sociosite/TOPICS>

Nonlibrary Sources

Interviews, questionnaires, surveys, and observation of the behavior of various groups and individuals are some of the important nonlibrary sources in social science research. Sometimes students conduct these types of research themselves. Sometimes professors provide unpublished results from these types of research that have been conducted by other students, the professor, colleagues of the professor, institutions, agencies, or research contractors. Assignments given by your professor may ask you to use your classmates as subjects for questionnaires. In political science, your teacher may ask you to interview a sample of college students and classify them as conservative, liberal, or radical. You may be asked to poll each group to find out college students' attitudes on nuclear energy, chemical waste disposal, the homeless, and other issues that affect them. If you were writing a paper on educational programs for gifted students, in addition to library research on the issue, you might want to observe two classes—one of gifted students and one of students not participating in the gifted program. You may also want to interview students, teachers, or parents. In psychology and social work, your research may rely on the observations of clients and patients and be written up as a case study (see p. 118).

Assignments in the Social Sciences

In many lower level social science courses, writing assignments take the same form as those in the humanities. However, as students progress into more highly specialized courses during the junior and senior years, they may very well receive assignments that require them to use formats used in the profession they plan to enter. Three of these types of writing are discussed here.

Proposals

Proposals, often the first stage of any research project, help to clarify and focus a research project.

In a proposal, your purpose is to persuade the recipient to grant your request. If an agency is to fund a proposed project, you have to sell its members on your idea. This means that you have to learn to put the purpose of your research project up front and support it. In the process, you must strictly adhere to the specifications outlined in the request for proposals issued by the grant-giving agency.

When an agency provides an RFP (Request for Proposals), it is important to follow the guidelines outlined in the RFP carefully and respond to all issues addressed in the RFP. Remember, priorities are given to proposals that focus on target areas identified in the RFP.

When an agency does not provide an RFP, use the following guidelines.

• **Cover Sheet:** State your name, the title of your project, and the name of the person or agency to whom your proposal is being submitted. Providing a short title will help you express your subject concisely. Thinking about the reader of your proposal will help you sharpen your focus. Usually, another line is added on this sheet that states the reason for the submission of the proposal—for example, a request for funding or facilities.

Advantages of the Maquiladora Project
in El Paso

Submitted to
The Committee on U.S.-Mexico Labor Relations
for
Grant to Research the Benefits of Maquiladora
Employment to El Paso

By Laura Talamantes

• **Abstract:** Usually on a separate page, the abstract provides a short summary of your proposal. (See p. 172 for information about writing abstracts.)

• **Statement of Purpose:** Essentially, this is your thesis statement. It states the purpose of your research project—for example, "The

Maquiladora Project is an industrial development program that relies on international cooperation with Mexican industries to use Mexican labor while boosting the employment of U.S. white collar workers."

- **Background of the Problem:** This section should explain why someone should spend time and money solving the problem you have identified. It is usually a paragraph that uses comparisons and contrasts with previous research and indicates the need for your specific research.

- **Rationale:** This section, which justifies further the need for your research project, should be as persuasive as you can make it. Why should the problem you have identified be solved? Why should the question you have posed be answered? Why is the solving of this problem and the answering of this question important at this time?

- **Statement of Qualification:** This section shows why you are qualified to carry out the needed research and what special qualities you bring to your work.

- **Literature Review:** This part can be a brief survey of the information you have looked at that justifies the need for your project and shows the uniqueness of your point of view. In a real-world proposal, this survey needs to be fairly complete, as it helps to establish the writer's credibility as a researcher. Many agencies have already paid for an extensive literature review. They may have identified problems from this literature.

- **Research Methods:** This paragraph describes the exact methods you will use in carrying out your research and the materials you will need. It enables the grantors to determine the soundness of your method.

- **Timetable:** Where applicable, the timetable states the time you will need to carry out the project.

- **Budget:** Where applicable, the budget estimates the costs for carrying out the research.

• **Conclusions:** This section restates the importance of your project.

• **Appendix:** This section contains support materials that would not be included in your text.

A proposal is usually sent with a cover letter, called a letter of transmittal, that follows business letter format. It is accompanied by a brief résumé, one that lists only your qualifications for the project. This résumé summarizes your relevant work experience and accomplishments, and it reinforces your qualifications as presented in the statement of qualification.

Case Studies

Case studies are usually informative, describing the problem at hand and presenting solutions or treatments. They all essentially follow the same format: the statement of the problem, the background of the problem, the methods or processes of the solutions, the conclusions arrived at, and suggestions for improvement or future recommendations. Different disciplines make different uses of case studies. In political science, deliberations in policy making and decision making are subject to the case study methodology. Foreign policy negotiations, for instance, are described and written up as case studies. Issue analyses such as "Should government control the media?" can also be written as case studies.

In psychology, social work, and educational psychology or counseling, the case study is an observation of an individual and his or her interaction with a certain agency. Such a case study usually involves describing the behavior of an individual or a group and outlining the steps to be taken in solving the problem that presents itself to the caseworker or researcher.

The case study that examines a problem in a group or in an environmental context follows the same format. Here is the introduction to a case study based on a social work student's assignment to observe one client.

Mona Freeman, a 14-year-old girl, was brought to the Denver Children's Residential Treatment Center by her 70-year-old, devoutly religious adoptive mother. Both were personable, verbal, and neatly groomed. The presenting problem was seen differently by various members of the client system: Mrs. Freeman described Mona's "several years of behavioral problems," including "lying, stealing and being boy crazy." Mona viewed herself as a "disappointment" and wanted "time to think." She had been expelled from the local Seventh-Day Adventist School for being truant and defiant several months earlier and had been attending public school. The examining psychiatrist diagnosed a conduct disorder but saw no intellectual, physical, or emotional disabilities. He predicted that Mona probably would not be able to continue to live in "such an extreme disciplinary environment" as the home of Mrs. Freeman because she had lived for the years from seven until twelve with her natural father in Boston, Massachusetts—a fact which was described as a "kidnapping" by Mrs. Freeman. The psychiatrist mentioned some "depression" and attributed it to Mona's inability to fit in her current environment and the loss of life with her father in Boston.

Journal Articles

• **Abstract:** This short summary appears first, but it is written last. (See p. 172.)

• **Literature Review:** This section includes a statement of the problem and summarizes relevant articles. It is funnel shaped in that it reviews many articles in a very brief space and ends with a sharp focus on the problem.

• **Research Methods:** The purpose of this section is to communicate exactly how you went about your research: description of sample, identification of instruments (interviews, observations, case study), itemization and explanation of procedures. This section should be so explicit that another researcher could replicate the study.

• **Findings:** This section communicates results. It clearly describes the answers to questionnaires, any observations, and test results. Frequently, these results are presented in tables or charts.

• **Discussion:** This section discusses the findings and relates the findings to the literature.

Conventions of Style and Format

Social science writing tends to use a technical vocabulary. For instance, in the social work case study, the student speaks of "the presenting problem," which is simply the reason the "subject," Mona, was brought to the Denver Children's Facility. Since you are speaking to specialists when you write papers in these disciplines, it is important to use the vocabulary of the field. Also, in describing charts and figures, it is important to use familiar statistical terms, such as *means, percentages, chi squares,* and other terms in the vocabulary of statistical analysis. But it is also important to explain in plain English what those percentages, means, and standard deviations mean in terms of your analysis.

The social science paper format typically uses internal headings (for example, Statement of Problem, Background of Problem, Description of Problem, Solutions, and Conclusion). Unlike the humanities paper, each section of a social science paper is written as a complete entity with a beginning and an end so that it can be read separately, out of context, and still make complete sense. The body of the paper may present charts or figures (graphs, maps, photographs, flow charts) as well as a discussion of those figures. Numerical data, such as statistics, are frequently presented in tabular form.

Documentation Formats

Documentation format in the social sciences is more uniform than in the humanities or the sciences. The disciplines and journals in the social sciences almost uniformly use the documentation style of the American Psychological Association's *Publication Manual.*

The APA Format*

APA format, which is used extensively in the social sciences, relies on short references—consisting of the last name of the author and the year of publication—inserted within the text. These references are keyed to an alphabetical list of references that follows the paper.

---

*APA documentation format follows the guidelines set in the *Publication Manual of the American Psychological Association.* 4th ed. Washington, DC: APA, 1994.

Parenthetical References in the Text

One author

The APA format calls for a comma between the name and the date, whereas MLA format does not.

```
One study of stress in the workplace (Weisberg,
1985) shows a correlation between ...
```

You should not include in the parenthetical reference information that appears in the text.

```
In his study, Weisberg (1983) shows a correlation
... (author's name in text)
```

```
In Weisberg's 1983 study of stress in the
workplace ... (author's name and date in text)
```

Two publications by same author(s), same year

If you cite two or more publications by the same author that appeared the same year, the first is designated *a*, the second *b* (e.g., Weisberg, 1983a; Weisberg, 1983b), and so on. These letter designations also appear in the reference list that follows the text of your paper.

```
He completed his next study of stress
(Weisberg, 1983b)....
```

A publication by two or more authors

When a work has two authors, both names are cited every time you refer to it.

```
There is a current and growing concern over the
use   of   psychological   testing   in   elementary
schools (Albright & Glennon, 1982).
```

If a work has three, four, or five authors, mention all names in the first reference, and in subsequent references cite the first author followed by *et al.* and the year (Sparks et al., 1984). When a work has six or more authors, cite the name of the first author followed by *et al.* and the year in first and subsequent references.

When citing multiple authors in the text of your paper, join the names of the last two with *and* (According to Rosen, Wolfe, and Ziff [1988] . . .). In parenthetical documentation, however, use an ampersand to join multiple authors (Rosen, Wolfe, & Ziff, 1988).

Specific parts of a source

When citing a specific part of a source, you should identify that part in your reference. APA documentation includes abbreviations for the words *page* ("p."), *chapter* ("chap."), and *section* ("sec.").

```
These theories have an interesting history
(Lee, 1966, p. 53).
```

Two or more works within the same parenthetical reference

List works by different authors in alphabetical order. Separate items with a semicolon.

```
... among several studies (Barson & Roth,
1985; Rose, 1987; Tedesco, 1982).
```

List works by the same author in order of date of publication.

```
... among several studies (Weiss & Elliot,
1982, 1984, 1985).
```

Distinguish works by the same author that appeared in the same year by designating the first *a*, the second *b*, and so on. (*In press* designates a work about to be published.)

```
... among several studies (Hossack, 1985a,
1985b, 1985c, in press).
```

Quotation

For a quotation, a page number appears in addition to the author's name and the year.

```
Because of information about Japanese success,
the United States has come to realize that
"Japanese    productivity    has    successfully
challenged, even humiliated, America in world
competition" (Bowman, 1984, p. 197).
```

The page number for a long quotation (40 words or more) also appears in parentheses but follows the period that ends the last sentence.

```
As Rehder (1983) points out, here women receive
    low wages, little job security, and less
    opportunity for training or educational
    development....
    (p. 43)
```

Listing the references

The list of all the sources cited in your paper falls at the end on a new numbered page with the heading *References.*

Items are arranged in alphabetical order, with the author's last name spelled out in full and initials only for the author's first and second names. Next comes the date of publication, title, and, for journal entries, volume number and pages. For books, the date of publication, city of publication, and publisher are included. Indent the first line of each entry five to seven spaces. Begin subsequent lines at the left margin.* Double space within and between entries.**

- **In the reference list**

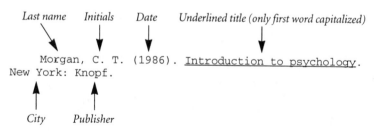

When determining the order of works in the reference list, keep the following guidelines in mind.

---

*The APA recommends this format for all manuscripts submitted for publication. If your instructor prefers, you may instead type the first line of each entry flush with the left margin and indent subsequent lines three spaces.

**Single spacing has been used in all APA examples to save space.

• Single-author entries precede multiple-author entries that begin with the same name.

```
Field, S. (1987) ...
Field, S., & Levitt, M. P. (1984) ...
```

• Entries by the same author or authors are arranged according to the year of publication, starting with the earliest date.

```
Ruthenberg, H., & Rubin, R. (1985) ...
Ruthenberg, H., & Rubin, R. (1987) ...
```

• Entries having the same author and date of publication are arranged alphabetically according to title. They include lowercase letters after the year.

```
Wolk, E. M. (1986a). Analysis ...
Wolk, E. M. (1986b). Hormonal ...
```

Sample Citations: Books

Capitalize only the first word of the title and the first word of the subtitle of books. Be sure to underline the title and to enclose in parentheses the date, volume number, and edition number. Separate major divisions of each entry with a period and one space.

A book with one author

```
    Maslow, A. H. (1974). Toward a psychology of
being. Princeton: Van Nostrand.
```

A book with more than one author

Notice that both authors are cited with last names first.

```
    Blood, R. O., & Wolf, D. M. (1960). Husbands
and wives: The dynamics of married living.
Glencoe: Free Press.
```

An edited book

> Lewin, K., Lippitt, R., & White, R. K. (Eds.).
> (1985). Social learning and imitation. New York:
> Basic Books.

A work in more than one volume

> Jones, P. R., & Williams, T. C. (Eds).
> (1990-1993). Handbook of therapy (Vols. 1-2).
> Princeton: Princeton University Press.

Note: The parenthetical citation in the text would be (Jones & Williams, 1990–1993).

A later edition

> Boshes, L. D., & Gibbs, F. A. (1972). Epilepsy
> handbook (2nd ed.). Springfield, IL: Thomas.

A book with a corporate author

> League of Women Voters of the United States.
> (1969). Local league handbook. Washington, DC:
> Author.

A book review

Place material that describes the form or content of the reference—review, interview, and so on—within brackets.

> Nagel, J. H. (1970). The consumer view of
> advertising in America [Review of Advertising in
> America: The consumer view] Personal Psychology
> 23, 133-134.

A translated book

> Carpentier, A. (1976). Reasons of state.
> (F. Partridge, Trans.). New York: W. W. Norton.

Sample Citations: Articles

Capitalize only the first word of the title and the first word of the subtitle of articles. Do not underline the article or enclose it in quotation marks. Give the journal title in full; underline the title and capitalize all major words. Underline the volume number and include the issue number in parentheses. Give inclusive page numbers. Separate major divisions of each entry with a period and one space.

An article in a scholarly journal with continuous pagination through an annual volume

```
     Miller, W. (1969). Violent crimes in city
gangs. Journal of Social Issues 27, 581-593.
```

An article in a scholarly journal that has separate pagination in each issue

```
     Williams, S., & Cohen, L. R. (1984). Child
stress in early learning situations. American
Psychologist, 21 (10), 1-28.
```

An encyclopedia article

```
     Hodge, R. W., & Siegel, P. M. (1968). The
measurement of social class. In D. L. Sills
(Ed.), International Encyclopedia of the Social
Sciences (Vol. 15, pp. 316-324). New York:
Macmillan.
```

A magazine article

Note: Use *p.* or *pp.* when referring to page numbers in magazines or newspapers *without* volume numbers. Omit the abbreviation for page numbers in referring to publications *with* volume numbers.

```
     Miller, G. A. (1984, November). The test:
Alfred Binet's method of identifying subnormal
children. Science, pp. 55-57.
     Hadingham, E. (1994, April). The Mummies of
Xinjiang. Discover, 15 (4),68-77.
```

A newspaper article

> Study finds many street people mentally ill.
> (1984, June 10). <u>New York Times</u>, p. A7.

> Boffy, P. M. (1982, January 24). Security and
> science collide on data flow. <u>New York Times</u>,
> p. A20.

An article in an edited book

> Tappan, P.W. (1980). Who is a criminal? In
> M. E. Wolfgang, L. Savitz, & N. Johnston (Eds.),
> <u>The sociology of crime and delinquency</u> (pp. 41-48).
> New York: Wiley.

A government publication

> National Institute of Mental Health.
> (1985). Television and the family: A report
> on the effect on children of violence and family
> television viewing, (DHHS Publication No. ADM
> 851274). Washington, DC: U.S. Government
> Printing office.

An abstract

> Pippard, J., & Ellam, L. (1981). Electro-
> convulsive treatment in Great Britain. <u>British
> Journal of Psychiatry, 139</u>, 563-568. (From
> <u>Psychological Abstracts</u>, 1982, <u>68</u>, Abstract
> No. 1567)

An interview

> Anderson, A., & Southern, T. (1958).
> (Interview with Nelson Algren]. In M. Cowley
> (Ed.), <u>Writers at work</u> (pp. 231-249). New York:
> Viking.

If the interview is not published, it does not appear in "References."
Instead, the text of the paper should clarify the interview's nature
and date. The same applies to other personal communications,
including letters and electronic messages.

Nonprint Sources

A film or videotape

> Kramer, S. (Producer), & Benedek, L. (Director).
> (1951). <u>Death of a salesman</u> (Film). Burbank: Columbia.

Electronic media

APA recommends the following generic formats for referring to on-line information:

> Author, I. (date). Title of article. Title
> of <u>Periodical</u> [on-line], xx. Available: Specific
> path
> Author, I. (date). Title of article.
> [CD-ROM]. <u>Title of Journal</u>, XX, XXX–XXX. Abstract
> from: Source and retrieval number.

Material from an on-line database

Enter material from an on-line database just as you would material from a portable database. Add the number of pages or paragraphs (if applicable), the name of the computer service or network, and the date of access.

> Epstein, W. M. (1996) Passing the proverbs.
> <u>Society</u>, 33:5, 19–23. Online.Internet. 3 Mar.
> 1998. Available: http://web4.searchbank.com/
> infotra...n/944/502/15063347w3/17!xrn_10&bkm

Material available only on-line

Enter the title, author, date of access and availability.

> The American Academy of Child and Adolescent
> Psychiatry. "Children & TV Violence" 6 May
> 1996. Available Internet: http://www.psych.
> med.umich.edu/web/aacap/factsfam/violence.
> htm.

Sample Student Papers in the Social Sciences

Two student papers follow. The first one, "Student Stress and Attrition," exemplifies the journal article format. The second one, "A Study of the Relationship of Maternal Smoking during Pregnancy to Low Birth Weight among Infants Born in a Massachusetts South Shore Hospital," exemplifies the research proposal. They both use APA documentation.

Sample
Social Science Paper
Journal Article
APA Format

Student Stress and Attrition

Gloria E. Medrano

University of Texas at El Paso

short title and number on every page

title repeated

Student Stress and Attrition

The National Center for Educational Statistics predicts an overall decrease of 7.5% in student enrollments between 1980 and 1988. This statistic translates into a decrease in undergraduate enrollments for four-year institutions of approximately 17%. This situation, coupled with present decreases in federal and state support for higher education, explains why 60% of the nation's college presidents agree that enrollment is a major concern (Dusek & Renteria, 1984).

interesting statistic for introduction

Ecklund and Henderson (1981), in their national longitudinal study of the high school class of 1972, documented how 43% of enrolling college freshmen had at one point or another dropped out of college. Thirty-four percent dropped out within their first two years (Ecklund & Henderson, 1981). The decreasing student populations and high dropout rates are directly affecting the state of our educational system. Although there is little that can be done about the lower numbers of incoming freshmen, something can be done to lessen the problem of college attrition.

author's name omitted from citation when it appears in sentence

The ideal approach to combatting this problem is to deal with the group of students closest in proximity to the university—the residence hall population. Many of their reasons for withdrawing from the university are traced to a fundamental cause: stress. In this case stress is the psychological

states thesis

phenomenon that contributes to the high
attrition rates of resident students.

Statement of the Problem

The on-campus resident student population
is very different from other groups of
individuals. They cannot be compared to such
groups as non-students, non-commuters, and
commuters. Aside from such student-related
stressors as academics and personal,
financial, and emotional problems, on-campus
resident students must also contend with
adjusting to their new environment, living
away from home and in a new community, having
a roommate, and being disturbed by the
overall noise level in the dormitories.

*distin-
guishes
and
classifies
the group
to be
studied*

Bishop and Snyder (1976) noted grades and
money as the major pressures that account for
the differences between residents and
commuters. Commuters ranked time management
next on their list, and residents listed
social pressures and concerns about their
future as their next most prominent problem.
Residents cited peer pressure more often as
sources of stress while commuters were more
concerned with difficulties of scheduling.

*year in
parentheses
—author's
name in
text*

Background of the Problem

Resident students at the University of
Texas at El Paso experience problems which
are different and distinct from other major
universities. of the more than 15,000 students
attending this university, slightly more than
700 live on campus. This is a relatively small

*background
of the group
to be
studied*

Student Stress 4

percentage compared to the neighboring campus
of New Mexico State University, where over
1,500 of the 12,000 students live on campus,
as stated by Richard Hanke in a personal
communication on December 2, 1984. U.T. El
Paso is a commuter campus, which means that
between 1 P.M. and 5 P.M. the campus is
virtually deserted. Many other universities,
like N.M.S.U., have campus-oriented
communities. The students have many
activities with which to fill their time. As
stated earlier, the social atmosphere is
directly related to student stress levels.
Many of our on-campus residents are from out
of town, with no means of transportation to
get them off campus, and there is no
immediate community around the campus. They
are therefore unable to expand their social
outlets. Another factor which relates to UTEP
is that many of our residents are freshmen;
they are often unfamiliar with many campus
activities that would serve to break the
monotony of campus living. Because of the low
numbers of on-campus residents and the high
numbers of commuting students, residents are
also limited in terms of the potential number
of people they can interact with.

use of comparison and contrast to highlight the problem

The new system of incorporating athletes
into the regular student housing system has
been particularly traumatic for non-athlete
residents. Previously, athletes were housed
in a separate dormitory, Burges Hall;
however, because that hall has fallen into
disrepair, the incoming freshmen football

Student Stress 5

players have been moved into Barry Hall's
third floor. This floor is between two other
non-academic floors. A non-academic floor is
one that is not especially designated for
honors students or other students requiring
special study hours. As such, non-academic
floors do not have designated quiet hours or
rules and regulations that foster study and
quiet. Aside from the usual noise related to
living in a non-academic dormitory,
additional problems, such as the dropping of
weights on the floor and disciplinary
problems related to the rowdiness of athletes
in general, also occur.

Description of the Problem

At the beginning of the fall semester of
1984, Barry Hall's second floor had
twenty-two residents. Three residents dropped
out of school because of personal and family
problems, and two residents moved to other
floors because of a roommate conflict that
could not be resolved. Of the remaining
seventeen residents, eleven will be returning
to the university in the spring semester.
Five students are leaving the system to study
at a university closer to home, and one is
moving out of the dormitory into an
apartment. Five of the returning students
will move back to Barry Hall's second floor,
while six will be moving to other floors
after having been seriously frustrated by
living on a nonacademic floor. This shows the
variety of different stressful situations
that can occur on a dormitory floor.

generalized description of the problem related to the specific case

Solutions

Although the dropout rate caused by stress in the dormitories does not significantly affect the university because most students are commuters, it is a problem which, if alleviated, will help to solve the institution's overall retention problem. At a time when UTEP is concerned with decreasing enrollments, maintaining enrollments is important. The implementation of a wide range of educational and social programming within the residence hall, strengthening the programs of recruitment, admission, counseling services, financial aid, career planning and placement, and health services will also contribute to decreased stress and improved retention.

It is imperative that those individuals who have the closest contact with the resident students—their resident assistants—be trained in handling stress. Additionally, they must be introduced thoroughly to the services available on campus. Resident assistants can work closely with, for instance, the New Students Relations office to point out incoming freshmen who might be prone to dropout. Resident assistants should also be involved in the workings of the freshmen orientation program and in other programs which can help students. These programs and departments include Financial Aid, the Career Information Center, Counseling Services, the Health Center, Placement Services, Student Association, and Study Skills.

Student Stress 6

Resident assistants should pay particular attention to their residents and watch for signs which warn them if students are having stress-related problems. If a resident assistant suspects that a resident is having a special problem, the resident can be referred to an appropriate program or department for help.

With proper training resident advisors can take the necessary steps to control the 50% attrition rates among on-campus resident students.

References

Bishop, J. B., & Snyder, G. S. (1976). Commuters and residents: Pressures, helps and psychological services. Journal of College Student Personnel, 17, 232-235.

Ecklund, B. K., & Henderson, L. B. (1981). Longitudinal study of the high school class of 1972. Washington, DC: National Institute of Education. (ERIC Document Reproduction Service No. ED 311 222).

Dusek, R., & Renteria, R. (1984, December 13). Plan slashes UTEP budget by 28%. El Paso Times, p. A1.

APA now recommends this format for all manuscripts submitted for publication. If your instructor prefers, you may type the first line of each entry flush with the left margin and indent each subsequent line three spaces.

Sample
Social Science Paper
Research Paper
APA Format

A study of the Relationship of
Maternal Smoking During Pregnancy
to Low Birth Weight Among Infants Born in a
Massachusetts South Shore Hospital

Debra K. White

Social Science 352

Dr. Robert Spiegel

December 12, 1994

Table of Contents

A Study of the Relationship of
Maternal Smoking During Pregnancy
to Low Birth Weight Among Infants Born in a
Massachusetts South Shore Hospital
Introduction

Problem

Physicians agree that low-birth-weight
babies, indicated by those weighing less than
5.5 pounds, struggle to survive their
infancy. These infants are 40 times more
likely to die during the first 4 weeks of
life than babies born over this weight
(Papalia & Olds, 1990:138). According to the
former Surgeon General, C. Everett Koop,
M.D., two-thirds of all babies who die in
their first year are low-birth-weight
infants.

The incidence of low birth weight is
recognized as a major public health concern.
When an infant is born with low birth weight,
it is more vulnerable to numerous
complications, many of which lead to death.
Those infants who do survive can be left with
disabling conditions, both physical and
psychological. Evidence of underdeveloped
lungs, more susceptibility to infections, low
blood sugar, jaundice, and bleeding in the
brain is found in low-birth-weight infants
(Papalia & Olds, 1990:138). In addition,
medical costs associated with treatment of
these and other complications are enormous.
Health insurance rates, for physicians and
individuals, have dramatically increased.
Answers to questions regarding the reduction

of risk factors attributable to low birth weight can have significant value to physicians, insurance companies, and the public.

Risk factors attributable to low birth weight can be demographic, socioeconomic, and associated with lifestyle. Lifestyle risk factors include poor nutrition, abuse of alcohol, and smoking. Previous research studies have concluded that there appears to be a relationship between these and other maternal risk factors and the delivery of low-birth-weight infants.

The present study will pursue the relationship of one particular lifestyle risk factor during pregnancy, smoking, to the incidence of low birth weight and attempt to confirm previous studies that a direct positive correlation between the two exists. Women who smoke during pregnancy are smoking for two. Through the placenta, the fetus receives toxic substances found in tobacco smoke. By smoking, the woman also reduces the oxygen supply to the fetus. When blood vessels in the placenta are restricted due to cigarette nicotine, nutrients to the fetus are reduced. Decreased oxygen and nutrients to the fetus reduce fetal growth. Pregnant women who smoke, therefore, are more likely to give birth to lower weight infants. If, on the other hand, pregnant women do not smoke, one can assume that they will be less likely to give birth to lower weight infants.

Amenability to Study

The relationship of maternal smoking during pregnancy to low-birth-weight infant is limited to bounds amenable to study. A review of the literature provides the theoretical framework for the present investigation. A combined population of pregnant women at different age, race, and economic levels as well as nurses and physicians is available and accessible for the study. Both probability/random and non-probability/non-random sampling procedures will be used to enumerate the appropriate number of respondents. The following major method will be used to ascertain the data from the prospective respondents: questionnaire. The obtained data will be critically analyzed by descriptive and inferential techniques.

Finally, time and funding are of minimal constraint in the present investigation, thus providing further evidence that the problem articulated above is limited to bounds amenable to study.

Significance of Study

The present study is significant from two perspectives: pure and applied. From the pure knowledge perspective, the findings of the present study will contribute to the existing literature in the following areas: health care, psychology, business, and education, among others. Furthermore, the results and conclusion generated by this study would help to develop a theoretical framework for further studies of the relationship of maternal smoking during pregnancy and the probability of low birth weight among infants.

From the applied perspective, the findings of the present study will help clarify the relationship of smoking during pregnancy to low birth weight. Expected results of the study show that mothers who smoke during pregnancy are more likely to give birth to low weight infants.

With this finding, programs can be developed to minimize low birth weight through smoking cessation. Physicians can educate pregnant women on the effects of their smoking and the consequences of delivering low-birth-weight babies, thus creating a motive for women to quit smoking during pregnancy. Decreasing the number of low-birth-weight infants can have a direct impact on medical costs and health insurance rates. Cessation programs and education would help limit the number of smoking pregnant women, thus reducing the number of low-birth-weight infants and increasing the survival rate of such infants.

Theoretical Framework
Review of Literature

A review of the literature suggests a positive correlation between smoking during pregnancy and low birth weight. In a recent study of women in Puerto Rico, Becerra and Smith (1988) attempted to examine the relationship of maternal smoking to low birth weight. They hypothesized that the effect of maternal smoking on birth weight is constant

among different socioeconomic and age groups
in Puerto Rico and that any effect of
smoking on birth weight is explained by
constitutional factors. To test their
assumptions, Becerra and Smith used secondary
analysis obtained from the Puerto Rico
Fertility and Family Planning Assessment
(PRFFPA). The sampling scheme of the PRFFPA
included a two-stage stratified cluster
sample representative of the entire
population of Puerto Rico. Questionnaires
were mailed to 4,500 households. A
representative sample of 3,175 women were
then interviewed. Respondents selected for
Becerra and Smith's study included singleton
births born in hospitals and whose birth
weights or birth dates were known. Becerra
and Smith focused on three questions that
defined the prenatal smoking exposure of
infants. The respondents were asked if they
currently smoked. If they answered, "yes,"
they were asked at what age they started
smoking. If they answered "no," they were
asked if they had ever been a cigarette
smoker. obtained data were analyzed by simple
descriptive techniques. Births to mothers who
started smoking regularly at some time before
delivery and who were still smoking at the
time of the interview were compared with
births to mothers who did not smoke. Becerra
and Smith reported that births to mothers who
smoked during pregnancy aged 20 and older
delivering in public hospitals were 2.5 times
more likely to weigh less than 2,500 grams
and on the average weighed 207 grams less

than births of a comparable group of non-smoking mothers (1988:268). The research concluded that there appears to be sufficient empirical evidence to support the assumption that maternal smoking is associated with an increased risk of low birth weight. Becerra and Smith's study provides an essential theoretical framework for the present investigation.

Similar conclusions were derived in a study conducted by a team of researchers at the Division of Nutrition (Fichtner, Sullivan, Zyrkowski, & Trowbridge, 1990). The researchers were interested in the relationship that smoking and other risk factors have to low birth weight. Nearly 248,000 records from the CDC's Pregnancy Nutrition Surveillance System (PNSS) were analyzed by the Division of Nutrition. Records that provided data on smoking; pregnancies that resulted in live, singleton births; and infant birth weight were used. Recorded smoking status was ascertained by asking the question, "Are you currently smoking cigarettes?" The data were analyzed by simple descriptive methods. The Division of Nutrition research team showed that the low-birth-weight percentage for smokers was 9.9 compared to 5.7 for nonsmokers (Fichtner et al., 1990:16). One weakness of the study, however, was that the prevalence of smoking is higher among PNSS participants than it is in the general population (Fichtner et al., 1990:17). Nevertheless, the research concluded that there appears to be a correlation between the risk factor, maternal smoking, and low birth weight.

Maternal smoking and its effect on birth weight were also studied by Sexton and Hebel (1984). Nine hundred thirty-five pregnant smokers from a large metropolitan area were randomly selected to participate in a clinical trial study. This study was conducted to test the hypothesis that a reduction in smoking during pregnancy would increase the birth weight of the infant. The women were randomly assigned to treatment and control groups. The intervention program was established and done primarily through individual contacts consisting of at least one personal visit and a monthly phone call. The percentage of women who reported not smoking cigarettes at the eighth-month contact was twice as high for the treatment group as for the control group, 43% and 20%, respectively (Sexton & Hebel, 1984:913). Hospital charts were used for the abstraction of birth-weight information. The data from the control group and treatment group were analyzed by one-way analysis of variance. Sexton and Hebel found for single, live births, the infants born to mothers in the treatment group had a mean birth weight of 3,278 grams, 92 grams heavier than the infants born to mothers in the control group and that the birth weight difference was statistically significant at P = < .05 (1984:913). Sexton and Hebel concluded that one of the major findings from their prospective, randomized, and controlled

experiment suggests that cessation even
during pregnancy improves the birth weight of
the baby (1984:914).

In another prenatal smoking cessation
study, Ershoff, Quinn, Mullen, and Lairson
(1990) arrived at similar conclusions. A
random sample of 323 smokers from five health
centers in southern California were assigned
to experimental and control groups.
Experimental subjects were introduced to a
serialized cessation program oriented to
women and pregnancy. All medical care
providers were blind to study group
assignment (Ershoff et al., 1990:342).
Hospital records were used to obtain birth
weight. The obtained data were analyzed by
using variance and covariance analysis. The
team of researchers found that women assigned
to the self-help cessation program were more
likely to give birth to infants weighing, on
average, 57 grams more than the infants born
to women in the control group, and were 45%
less likely to deliver a low-birth-weight
infant (Ershoff et al., 1990:340). The
researchers concluded that there is strong
evidence that supports a relationship between
maternal smoking cessation and increasing
birth weight.

In a final study reviewed, Shiono,
Klebanoff, and Rhoads (1986) were interested
in smoking and alcohol use during pregnancy
and their effect an preterm births. (Preterm
births have been associated with low birth
weight in other studies.) The 30,598 women in
the study were recruited from 13 Kaiser

clinics serving northern California. As part
of their prenatal care at Kaiser, the women
had completed self-administered
questionnaires that included information on
their use of tobacco and alcohol. Kaiser's
computerized records were used to obtain
pregnancy outcomes. Multiple linear logistic
regression was used to estimate the adjusted
odds ratios for preterm (<37 weeks) and very
preterm (<35 weeks) births. The researchers
found that preterm births were 20% more
common in women smoking at least one pack of
cigarettes per day, and the strongest effect
was seen in very preterm births in whom the
excess was 60% (Shiono et al., 1386:82). The
study suggests that smoking during pregnancy
leads to preterm birth.

Hypothesis

In view of the above discussions and the
review of the literature, the present study
will attempt to provide empirical support to
the thesis that mothers who smoke during
pregnancy are more likely to give birth to
low-weight infants. In other words, the
present study will provide evidence to
support the view that fetuses exposed to
smoke will weigh less at birth than fetuses
who have not been exposed.

Operational Definitions

Concepts used in the hypothesis statement
have been operationally defined, in that they
have been reduced to the level where they can
be measured empirically. Formerly, mothers
who smoked during pregnancy were defined as
pregnant women who inhaled tobacco smoke.

operationally, this concept will be measured by the following indices: Any pregnant woman between the ages of 18 and 40 years, who was a prepregnant smoker and who continued to smoke at the time of delivery a minimum of one pack of cigarettes per week. The dependent variable, low birth weight in infants, is formally defined as a weight less than 5.5 pounds (2,500 grams) at birth (Papalia & Olds, 1990:137). Operationally, low birth weight in infants will be measured in pounds and ounces and converted to grams. Only singleton births whose birth weights are between 1,000 and 2,000 grams will be included in the analysis.

Assumptions, Limitations, and Delimitations

The major theoretical assumption guiding the present investigation is that toxic substances in tobacco smoke pass through the placenta of a pregnant woman and reach her developing fetus. If the fetus is exposed to these toxic substances, then there will be some adverse physiological change that will manifest in the newborn. However, if on the other hand, the fetus is not exposed to toxic substances, then it will not have the adverse physiological change in birth weight. More specifically, the assumption is that the birth weight of newborns will be lower if the mother smokes during pregnancy.

Time and funding will place several limitations upon the present study, among which are the following:

1. Small sample size
2. Not as comprehensive as a study could be
3. Restriction on the number of hospitals or clinics to be investigated

Other limitations reflect the homogeneous nature of the sample that may not lend itself to generalization beyond the sample studied. The sample will be selected from a white, middle-class community in the South Shore area of Massachusetts. Respondents will be selected from only one hospital, and thus will not be considered a representative sample of the community. No information regarding socioeconomic status, race, health education, time that prenatal care began, drinking during pregnancy, family background and history, and subjectivity to passive smoke will be available, thus limiting the ability of the present investigation to control intervening or extraneous variables. In view of the above limitations, the major delimitation of the present study is its inability to generalize the major finding and conclusions beyond the sample population under scrutiny.

Methodology

Nature and Design of Study

The present study is descriptive in nature. A descriptive study is the "defining and classifying of events and their relationships" (Bootzin & Acocella, 1988:116). More specific to the present study, attempts will be made to describe the relationship of maternal smoking to the incidence of low birth weight.

The design of the present study is cross-sectional. Papalia and Olds define a cross-sectional study as "research that assesses different people of different ages at the same time" (1990:40). Specifically, the present study will assess women who gave birth during the spring of 1991. The present investigation will be conducted in a community with a total population of 20,000 people and located in the southeastern part of Massachusetts.

Sampling Procedure

Selecting a sample is predicated upon a number of factors, among which include the availability, accessibility, receptivity, and special qualifications of the prospective respondents. In view of the above constraints, the present study will use a random sampling procedure. More specifically, a simple random sample will be used to enumerate the appropriate pregnant women for the present investigation. In a simple random sample, a number is assigned to each population member; and using a table of random numbers, selections are made until the number of individuals needed for the study have been reached (Sanders & Pinhey, 1987:114-115).

For the present study, all women who had already given birth constitute the population of the study. The investigator will meet with four obstetricians of a South Shore hospital and discuss with them the proposed study. Upon the approval of the obstetricians, the investigator will receive a list of the names

of women who gave birth during the spring of
1991. The next step would be to assign a
number to each woman. Using a table of random
numbers, 50 women from each list supplied by
the four obstetricians will be selected. A
total of 200 women will constitute the sample
size.

Methods of Data Collection

Data needed to complete the present study
will be obtained from the respondents by a
survey method, specifically, a questionnaire.
This particular method of data collection
offers advantages over other methods:

1. Permits wide coverage for minimum expense
2. Permits more considered answers
3. Gives respondents a sense of privacy
4. Greater uniformity in the manner in which
   questions are posed
5. Provides responses that are easier to
   quantify than observations made in
   interviews

The questionnaire is designed in such a
manner as to facilitate collection of data in
the following areas:

1. Demographic characteristic: age of
   pregnant woman
2. Independent variable: smoking behavior of
   the woman before and during pregnancy
3. Dependent variable: birth weight of baby
   born to pregnant woman

A pretested questionnaire with a cover
letter and a self-addressed stamped envelope
will be mailed to each mother. The mother

will be asked to complete the questionnaire
and return it to the investigator by the
deadline specified in the cover letter. A
follow-up postcard will be mailed out to each
mother thanking her for her cooperation in
completing the study. Furthermore, a
follow-up postcard promises to increase the
number of returns.

Method of Data Analysis

Once all the questionnaires to be included
in the analysis have been received, the first
step in the analysis will be to tally all
responses to each questionnaire item. Next,
the questionnaire will be categorized into
one of two groups:

1. Women who smoked during pregnancy
2. Women who did not smoke during pregnancy

Each respondent will be further classified
into one of two groups:

1. women giving birth to low-birth-weight
   infants (weighing less than 2,500 grams)
2. Women giving birth to non-low-birth-weight
   infants (weighing more than 2,500 grams)

Major relationships to be analyzed include
the following:

1. Relationship of respondents to:
   a. smoking during pregnancy
   b. nonsmoking during pregnancy
2. Relationship of respondents to:
   a. giving birth to low-birth-weight
      infants
   b. giving birth to non-low-birth-weight
      infants

3. Relationship of smoking and nonsmoking
   during pregnancy to:
   a. low-birth-weight infants
   b. non-low-birth-weight infants

The relationship of the independent variable
(smoking) and the dependent variable (low
birth weight) will assume the following
two-by-two format:

	Low Birth Weight		
Smoking	Yes	No	Total
Yes	___	___	___
No	___	___	___
Total	___	___	___

   Phi coefficient will be used to measure the
association between smoking and low birth
weight. Finally, chi-square test statistics
will be used to test the null hypothesis of
no difference between smoking and low birth
weight.

<u>Reliability and Validity</u>

   Reliability is concerned with consistency.
If an instrument or a study consistently
yields the same result, then the instrument
or the study is said to possess reliability.
Because the present study will not be
repeated over a period of time, it would be
somewhat problematic to establish its
reliability. However, the pretested
instrument of the present study would assure,
at least to some extent, a measure of
reliability of the present investigation.

The present study possesses face validity. By the professional judgment of the investigator, the present proposed study is said to possess validity. The present investigation is derived from an extensive review of the literature. The hypothesis and the operational definitions have sound theoretical underpinnings, thus assuring construct/external validity. Finally, the instrument has been pretested, contributing to the internal/content validity of the present study.

In summary, then, the present investigation is said to possess not only reliability but also validity.

References

Becerra, J. E., & Smith, J. C. (1988). Maternal smoking and low birth weight in the reproductive history of women in Puerto Rico, 1982. <u>American Journal of Public Health</u>, 78, 268-272.

Bootzin, R. R., & Acocella, J. R. (1988). <u>Abnormal psychology: Current perspectives</u> (5th ed.). New York: Random House.

Ershoff, D. H., Quinn, V. P., Mullen, P. D., & Lairson, D. R. (1990). Pregnancy and medical cost outcomes of a self-help prenatal smoking cessation program in an HMO. <u>Public Health Reports</u>, 105(4), 340-347.

Fichtner, R. R., Sullivan, K. M., Zyrkowski, C. L., & Trowbridge, F. L. (1990). Racial/ethnic differences in smoking, other risk factors, and low birth weight among low-income pregnant women, 1978-1988. <u>Morbidity and Mortality Weekly Report,</u> 39 (SS-3), 13-21.

Fox, S. H., Brown, C., Koontz, A. M., & Kessel, S. S. (1987). Perceptions of risks of smoking and heavy drinking during pregnancy: 1985 NHIS findings. <u>Public Health Reports</u> <u>102(1),</u> 73-79.

Monette, D. R., Sullivan, T. J., & DeJong, C. R. (1990). Applied social research: Tool for the human services (2nd ed.). Fort Worth: Holt, Rinehart and Winston.

Papalia, D. E., & Olds, S. W. (1990). A child's world: Infancy through adolescence (5th ed.). New York: McGraw-Hill.

Sanders, J., & Pinehy, A. (1983). The conduct of social research. New York: Holt, Rinehart and Winston.

Sexton, M., & Hebel, J. R. (1984). A clinical trial of change in maternal smoking and its effect on birth weight. Journal of the American Medical Association, 255 (7), 911-915.

Shiono, P. H., Klebanoff, M. A., & Rhoads, G. G. (1986). Smoking and drinking during pregnancy. Journal of the American Medical Association, 255 (1), 82-84.

U.S. Department of Health and Human Services (USDHHS). (1985). Smoking and pregnancy (DHHS Publication No. 85-89-P). Washington, DC: Government Printing Office.

APA now recommends this format for all manuscripts submitted for publication. If your instructor prefers, you may use hanging indents. See page 123.

Maternal Smoking 21

Appendix

Maternal Smoking 22

2 Thoreau Drive
South Easton, MA 02375
November 1, 1994

Dear Respondent's Name:

I am a student at Stonehill College and am presently conducting a research study in partial fulfillment of the requirements for my degree. This study involves an analysis of smoking during pregnancy.

Dr. Michael Baines, Chief of Obstetrics and Gynecology, has granted me permission to conduct this research among the patients of all four obstetricians at BYU Hospital. A random sample of fifty patients from each of the four obstetricians has been selected for this study. I am happy to inform you that you were randomly selected as a subject in this scientific research investigation.

Please complete the attached questionnaire and return it in the self-addressed stamped envelope no later than December 28, 1994. Please be assured that no respondent will be personally identified in this study and that the information you provide me will be treated with the utmost confidentiality.

If you have any questions, either about the study or the attached questionnaire, please feel free to call me at (508) 238-1135 and I will be happy to answer them.

Thank you for your consideration. If you desire a copy of the study results/findings, please let me know and I will be most happy to provide you with a copy.

Sincerely,
Debra K. White

QUESTIONNAIRE

Please complete this questionnaire by checking the appropriate responses or by providing the needed information. Your candor is crucial to this study.

1. Are you currently a smoker?

_____ YES   _____ NO

2. Did you smoke prior to your pregnancy?
_____ YES   _____ NO

If you answered yes to question number 2, on the average, how much did you smoke prior to your pregnancy?

_____ Less than one pack of cigarettes per day

_____ One or more packs of cigarettes per day

3. Did you smoke during your pregnancy?

_____ YES   _____ NO

If you answered yes to question number 3, on the average, how much did you smoke during your pregnancy?

_____ Less than one pack of cigarettes per day

_____ One or more packs of cigarettes per day

4. Did you deliver:

_____ singleton birth (one baby)

_____ multiple birth (two or more babies)

IF YOU HAD A SINGLETON BIRTH PLEASE ANSWER ALL
OF THESE QUESTIONS. IF YOU HAD A MULTIPLE
BIRTH PLEASE GO DIRECTLY TO QUESTION 8.

5. Sex of your baby: _____ Male _____ Female

6. Length of infant at birth _____ Inches

7. Weight of infant at birth

_____ Pounds _____ Ounces

8. How old were you at the time of delivery?

_____ Years

If you have any additional information about
this study and/or if you wish to comment on
this study, please do so here:

WRITING IN THE SCIENCES

The natural sciences include fields such as astronomy, biology, chemistry, geology and physics. Essentially two types of writing are used in the sciences, literature reviews and research papers. Literature reviews report and summarize on the work that others have done, whereas research papers report one's own work. The format for literature reviews is common to the reports and reviews of other subjects. The research paper format, on the other hand, follows a traditional format that illuminates the work done, the data gathered, how they were analyzed and, finally, the conclusion(s) drawn from the study. Writing is an integral part of a scientist's career. Correspondence, research papers, articles, and grants are used to disseminate their discoveries to other researchers and funding agencies in the hope of receiving recognition for the work done and monetary support for further studies or experimentation. In addition to being technical and concise, scientific writing should be precise and clear, relating information accurately and allowing the work to be reproduced by you or others exactly as it had been conducted in the past.

Research Sources

The work of a scientist is done not only in the field or laboratory but also in the library. Prior to conducting a study or experiment, information relevant to the project must be gathered and analyzed to determine what has been done, what should be repeated, and what needs to be done. The formidable task of combing through the wealth of information available on a topic is made easier by using general and specific reference sources and computer databases.

Specialized Library Sources

The library contains many reference sources, which can be valuable in the research done in the preparation for either writing a paper or performing a study. The following sources are grouped by discipline:

General Science

Applied Science and Technology Index
CRC Handbook of Chemistry and Physics
  (and other titles in the CRC series of handbooks)
General Science Index
McGraw-Hill Encyclopedia of Science and Technology
Science Citation Index

Chemistry

Analytical Abstracts
Chemical Abstracts
Encyclopedia of Chemistry
Kirk-Othmer Encyclopedia of Chemical Technology

Engineering

Engineering Encyclopedia
Engineering Index
Environment Index
Government Reports Announcements (NTIS)
HRIS Abstracts (Highway Engineering)
Internet Engineering Task Force (IETF)
Requests for Comments (RFC)

Geology

Abstracts of North American Geology
Annotated Bibliography of Economic Geology
Bibliography and Index of Geology
Bibliography of North American Geology
GeoAbstracts (Geographical Abstracts)
Publications of the USCS
Selected Water Resources Abstracts

Life Sciences

> *Biological Abstracts*
> *Biological and Agricultural Index*
> *Encyclopedia of Bioethics*
> *Encyclopedia of the Biological Sciences*
> *Index Medicus*

Mathematics

> *Index to Mathematical Papers*
> *Mathematical Reviews*
> *Universal Encyclopedia of Mathematics*

Physics

> *Astronomy and Astrophysics Abstracts*
> *Encyclopedia of Physics*
> *Physics Abstracts*
> *Solid State Abstracts Journal*

Specialized Databases for Computer Searches

As in other disciplines, powerful on-line or CD-ROM databases have made searching a topic much easier. The popularity of these databases stems from their ease of operation, flexible search routines that allow both very narrow and very broad searches, and speed. Useful science databases are

Agricola	*Entrez*	*NTIS*
BIOSIS Previews	*Inspec*	*SCISEARCH*
CAB Abstracts	*Life Sciences Collection*	*World Wide Web*
CASearch	*MATHSCI*	
Compendex	*MEDLINE*	

The World Wide Web (www) contains a wealth of information that can be of great value for researching a particular topic. However, it must be kept in mind that just about anyone can put just about anything on the Web. Therefore, it is strongly recommended that only reliable Web sites be used as sources of information. The following are Web sites for various disciplines within the sciences, any one of which can serve as a good starting point, since they contain links to other valuable and relevant sites within the given discipline.   `·`

Biology:
<http://golgi.harvard.edu/biopages.html>

Chemistry:
<http://www.chem.ucla.edu/chempointers.html>

Engineering:
<http://arioch.gsfc.nasa.gov/wwwvl/engineering.html>

Mathematics:
<http.euclid. math. fsu.edu/Science/math.html>

Physics:
<http://www.w3.org/vl/Physics/Overview.html>

Psychology:
<http://www-mugc.cc.monash.edu.au/psy/ol/psylinks.html>

Laboratory and Field Sources

Most scientists spend their time in the laboratory, but some may spend most of their time in the field. The laboratory can vary from a room within a modern building to a tent in the middle of the Brazilian rain forest. What is necessary is that the facility have the materials and equipment essential to conducting experiments and collecting data. The field, or area being studied, is defined differently, depending upon the type of research being conducted. For the ecologist it may be a pond; for an agronomist, a farmer's field; for a clinical chemist, a hospital; for a microbiologist, a water treatment facility; for a geologist, the Grand Canyon; or for a volcanologist, Mount St. Helen. Experimentation, sample and data collection, and analyses can be performed in both the field and the laboratory.

Assignments in the Sciences

The science student will most often be assigned to write either a report of his or her own work performed in the laboratory or a review of a particular subject area. Laboratory reports, written at the completion of one or more related lab exercises or a research project in a laboratory-based science course, often share the scientific article format but are less formal and rigorous in their requirements. The second form of a scientific paper, the review, surveys a collection of related primary sources. Primary scientific literature can be found in scholarly journals. A review is an example of secondary scientific literature. Primary literature often is intended for a specialized audience with a fair degree of background knowledge, whereas secondary literature is geared toward a more general audience. That being the case, the more general scientific writing assignments will be discussed first, followed by those that are more specific.

Literature Reviews

A literature review examines a collection of primary literature related to a particular topic. The previously mentioned indices, abstracts, and databases are of tremendous help in selecting sources appropriate for a given topic. Once the relevant articles have been collected, they should be read carefully, and notes should be taken meticulously. The paper should open with a paragraph, known as an abstract, that clearly indicates the paper's intent and progress from that point to coherently express the important information that has been learned. Bits of information should be tied together so that they progress in a logical manner and be supported with proper documentation. Understanding of the material is demonstrated by relating critical experiments, their results and importance to the purpose of the study, as well as comparing and contrasting the works being studied rather than simply providing individual summaries of the papers. In science, the use of one's own words is preferable to the use of direct quotations.

Laboratory Reports/Research Papers

Laboratory reports and research papers convey information about a select set of experiments or studies that have been conducted by the author(s). The report states the significance of the study's results within the context of what was known previously. Most published research papers have a traditional format (discussed in the following section). The intent of the paper or report is to communicate a set of information that has been gained through investigative research. This information is presented so that the reader understands what was done, what data were gathered, how they were analyzed, and how they were interpreted.

Conventions of Style and Format

There is a traditional format for a scientific paper based on the logic of the scientific method and argument. There are eight parts to the paper: *Title, Abstract, Introduction, Materials and Methods, Results, Discussion, Acknowledgments,* and *Literature Cited.* A description of each section follows.

Title. The last part of the paper to be written is actually the first that a reader would encounter—the title. Three adjectives should be kept in mind when you are deciding on the title of a research paper or laboratory report: *informative, specific* and *concise.* The decision as to whether additional time should be spent reading the paper is often determined by the title. Therefore, the title should contain key words that identify the goal or the most important information that was gained from the study.

Abstract. This is a single, concise (the length is often limited to 250 words) paragraph, written in the active voice, that summarizes the paper. Clearly stated is the reason for the work, how it was done, and the conclusions that were made. The abstract states the important points made in the paper and thereby allows people to assess whether the contents of the paper are relevant to their research. It is usually easiest to write the following four sections of the paper before writing the abstract.

Introduction. This section is usually no longer than a few paragraphs and provides several important pieces of information. The original work that is the focus of the article is placed into context by reviewing the problem being addressed, its importance, and relevant background information. The introduction should make the following points clear: the purpose of the study, what is to be learned from it, and the approach the authors have taken to obtain the new information. Most often the introduction will be written so that it leads up to the goals of the investigation, which are stated last in this section.

Materials and Methods. This section is usually the easiest to write. It provides a description of the equipment, supplies, organisms/test subjects and procedures used in the investigation and analysis of the data. The information should be clearly written and contain sufficient detail to allow another researcher to reproduce the work as it was conducted originally. When a particular material or method has been previously described in a widely available journal, then a citation should be given in place of a detailed description.

Results. This section is often a combination of text and illustration used to present the results of the study, and there should be no interpretation. For clarity the data should be organized and represented in the form of a graph, chart, table, or figure that will have to be cited in the text. Any figures should be located as close as possible to its reference in the text, be labeled with a heading (Table I or Figure 1), and contain a legend that describes its contents.

Discussion. This is where the results are summarized and thoughtfully interpreted. This section should discuss whether the findings of the investigation support the hypothesis and goals of the study. Keep in mind that a scientific argument is being constructed; therefore, the discussion should be written with confidence and demonstrate logic, with each point that is made supported by one or more pieces of evidence. The discussion should focus on specifics and contain explanations that are solidly constructed on the interpretations of the data. It is also appropriate in this section to discuss future investigations based upon the knowledge gained from the study.

Acknowledgments. Credit or appreciation is given in this section to those who assisted in or provided a service to the study. Those mentioned may be individuals who supplied samples, suggested methods for assessment of data, critically read the manuscript prior to its submission, or funded the research.

Literature Cited. This section is merely a listing of the sources referred to in the body of the paper. Only the sources cited in the paper should be included in this section. Any sources not referenced in the paper, but which may be relevant to the subject matter, of interest to the reader, or consulted but not used in writing the paper, should not be listed in this section. Various formats (discussed in the following section) are used to document the sources in both the body of the paper and the literature cited section.

Documentation Formats

The professional societies of certain science disciplines have published their own style manuals that provide citation and reference list formats. References within a paper can be found in two locations: within the text and in the literature cited section. The complete reference in the literature cited section provides the necessary information for a person to retrieve the referred source. The following material outlines the citation methods and reference formats used in the sciences.

Manuals for Style and Format

There is no standard format for citing sources within a paper or listing references in the literature cited section of a scientific paper. However, style and format manuals for various science disciplines are available from the appropriate professional societies.

Biology:

Council of Biology Editors Style Manual Committee. (1994) *Scientific style & format: the CBE manual for authors, editors, & publishers.* 6th ed. Northbrook, IL: Council of Biology Editors, Inc.

Atlas, M. C. (1995) *Author's handbook of styles for life science journals.* CRC Press, Inc.

Chemistry:

The American Chemical Society. (1997) Dodd, J. S. ed. *The ACS Style Guide: A Manual for Authors and Editors.* 2nd ed. Washington, DC: The American Chemical Society.

Mathematics:

> Krantz, S. G. (1997) *A primer of mathematical writing.* Providence, RI: American Mathematical Society.

Medicine:

> American Medical Association (1997) *American Medical Association manual of style: a guide for authors & editors.* 9th ed. Baltimore, MD: Williams & Wilkins.
>
> Huth, E. J. (1990) *How to write & publish papers in the medical sciences.* 2nd ed. Baltimore, MD: Williams & Wilkins.
>
> Huth, E. J. (1989) *Medical style & format: an international manual for authors, editors & publishers.* Baltimore, MD: Williams & Wilkins.

Physics:

> American Institute of Physics. (1990) *Style manual.* 4th ed. College Park, MD: AIR

Psychology:

> American Psychological Association. (1994) *Publication manual of the American Psychological Association.* Washington, DC: American Psychological Association.

Citing Sources in the Text

A citation in the body of a paper indicates that the information is not common knowledge or an original thought or idea. To use information from another source without proper acknowledgment of the source is plagiarism and illegal, not to mention unethical. The citation itself should either precede or follow the material to be referenced. In the sciences, the two formats used to cite sources within the text are the *name-year* and *number* formats. The format used will depend upon the preferences of the journal or course instructor to whom the paper will be submitted.

Name-Year Format

The name-year format identifies a specific reference, using the last name of the first author and the year the source was published. There are two ways of doing this:

(1) The name and year are provided within parentheses following the information derived from the source. Note that the name and year may or may not be separated by a comma.

> . . . is an appropriate gene replacement method (Almeida, 1996). The use of transposons . . .

(2) If the name of the author appears in the sentence itself, then only the date is placed within parentheses

> . . . wide range of problems in biology. Almeida (1996) was the first to use . . .

- If a cited work has two authors, then both last names should be provided.

> . . . b-amyloid protein precursor (Daigle and Li, 1993). Plaques found in . . .

- If a cited work has three or more authors, then the abbreviation *et al.* (from the Latin phrases *et alii* or *et alia* meaning "and others") is included (note that *"et al."* should be either italicized or underlined to indicate a foreign language):

> . . . banding patterns were identical (Denome et al., 1994). The ability to characterize . . .

- If there are two or more sources by the same author(s), list the publication dates in chronological order.

> . . . dependent upon transposon activity (Eide and Anderson, 1985, 1988). Indicative of . . .

- If there are two or more sources by the same author(s) published within the same year, the dates should be followed by lowercase letters that also must appear in the reference list:

> . . . were statistically relevant. Solomon et al., (1990a, 1990b) state that FHC is . . .

- If there are two or more sources by different authors, arrange them in chronological order and use a semicolon to separate works by separate authors:

> . . . myosin heavy chain (McKenna and Watkins, 1981; Rayment et al., 1993, 1995). The hypertrophy of the myocardium is . . .

- If there are two or more sources with the authors sharing the last name, include their initials and arrange them in alphabetical order based on the initials:

  . . . in the analysis of DNA (Denome, R.M., 1994; Denome, S.A. 1994). From these data . . .

- If the source is from a book that has an editor and contains a collection of works by different authors, provide only the name of the author(s) of the particular work within the collection and the publication date for the collection:

  . . . of C. elegans muscle ultrastructure (Waterston, 1988). Pennate-fiber muscle is . . .

- If the source is unpublished and has been distributed in class (*e.g.,* a handout or laboratory manual written by an instructor), provide the instructor's name and the year:

  . . . as described in the lab manual (Almeida, 1997). Each column fraction was . . .

- If the source is a publication or an organization and does not specify an author, provide the name of the organization followed by the publication date:

  . . . understanding through exploration (South Carolina Department of Education, 1996).

- If citing information obtained through a method of personal communication such as a conversation or letter, include the words "pers. comm." (Note: persons being referenced in this manner should give their permission, and these citations should not be listed in the literature cited section since they are not easily accessible.):

  . . . mutant phenotype (Waterston, pers. comm.). Enhancer analysis may identify . . .

- If citing information from the World Wide Web, provide the author(s) name(s) and the date of publication or last revision:

  . . . in development or clinical trials (AIDS Action Committee of Massachusetts, Inc., 1998).

Number Format

In the number system each reference is assigned a number that is inserted at a citation point. The number can be either in parentheses or superscripted. The numbers are assigned by either the order of the references as they first appear in the paper or by their alphabetical listing in the literature cited section.

Multiple sources are separated by commas; however if three or more references are consecutive, the numbers of the first and of the last references are given and are separated by a hyphen:

- citation within parentheses:

    . . . thick and thin filaments. (21, 33–37, 42)

- citation superscripted:

    . . . thick and thin filaments. 21, 33–37, 42

Listing Sources in the Literature Cited Section

Many times a person may want to obtain the original work cited in a paper. The information provided in the citation will lead to a complete reference for the work in the literature cited section. For this reason all sources provided in the body of the paper must have a complete reference. A complete reference provides the information necessary to obtain the original work that has been cited in the paper.

Components of a Complete Citation

There is a minimum amount of information needed to trace a body of work: the last name and first and middle initials (if provided) of the author(s); the publication date; the title of the publication; and the volume and page numbers. If a publication does not number the pages consecutively from one issue to the next within a single volume, then the issue number should also be provided. Additional information often provided is the title of the journal article or chapter within a book, the place of publication and editor, if there is one. In the sciences there is no set format for a reference. The styles used vary within disciplines and among scientific journals. Exact formatting guidelines for the literature cited section (and the remainder of the paper as well) can be obtained from the instructor of the course for which the paper is being written, the style manual published by the professional society of the discipline in which the paper is being written, or the journal to which a paper is to be submitted. The following examples are not meant to represent an exhaustive list of accepted styles. These examples provide general formats that may be modified by rearrangement of the order of some of the components (the location of the publication date), as well as inclusion or exclusion of parentheses, periods, commas, colons, use of italics etc.

- Always include the last name and first and middle initials of all authors with each author's name separated from another's by a comma. Use standard abbreviations for journal titles or write out the entire title:

  Sweeney, H. L., Straceski, A. J., Leinwand, L. A., Tikunov, B. A. and Faust, L. (1994) Heterologous expresssion of a cardiomyopathic myosin that is defective in its actin interaction. *J. Biol. Chem.* 269: 1603–1606.

- When the reference cited has been accepted for publication by a journal but has not been published yet, it should be noted as "in press."

  Glasner, J., Kocher, T., and Collins, J. *Caenorhabditis elegans* contains genes encoding both dimeric and tetrameric types of alcohol dehydrogenase. *J. Molec. Evol.* (in press).

- Italicize book names; include place of publication and the edition number if the source is a second edition or higher:

  Alberts, B., Bray, D., Lewis, J., Raff, M., Roberts, K., and Watson, J. D. (1994) *Molecular Biology of the Cell,* 3rd ed. New York, NY: Garland Publishing, Inc.: 849–851.

- The reference for an edited book should provide the name or names of the editor(s):

  McKenna, W. J., and Watkins, H. C. Hypertrophic cardiomyopathy. In: Scriver, C. R., Beaudet, A. L., Sly, W. S., and Valle, D. eds. *The metabolic and molecular bases of inherited diseases.* 7th ed. Vol. 3 New York, NY: McGraw Hill, 1995: 4253–72.

- If the source is unpublished course material, provide the name of the school and the state in which it is located in place of the publishing information:

  Almeida, C. A. (1997) *BI 215 research methods laboratory manual.* Stonehill College, Easton, MA: 21–25.

- To reference an internet source provide the name of the author(s), the year the information was made accessible, the title, the complete URL of the web page in angle brackets, and the date the information was accessed:

  Casey, D. and Martin, S. (1997) Education and the Human Genome Project. < http://www.ornl.gov/TechResources/Human_Genome/resource/education.html> (December 30, 1997)

- A reference to an e-mail message provides the name of the sender, his or her e-mail address in angle brackets, the date the e-mail message was sent, the subject line, the type of communication in square brackets, and the date on which the e-mail message was accessed.

  Parham, C. <parham@dnax.org> (April 20, 1997) Stock center mutants [Personal e-mail] (April 21, 1997).

Arrangement of Citations by Last Name or Number

References can be listed by alphabetical order according to the last name of the primary author of each reference whether or not the name-year or number system is used as a citation method. The alphabetical listing of references is numbered consecutively for the number system, and those numbers are inserted at a citation point. Alternatively, the citations can be numbered in the order in which they appear in the text of the paper and then arranged numerically in the literature cited section. The following are some guidelines for the listing of references alphabetically.

- If there are at least two sources with the same author(s) published within the same year, the dates should be followed by lower case letters:

  Solomon, S. D., Geisterfer-Lowrance, A. A. T., Vosberg, H. P., Hiller, G., Jarcho, J. A., Morton, C. C., McBride, W.O., Mitchell, A. L., Bale, A. E., McKenna, W. J., Seidman, J. G., and Seidman, C. E.

(1990a) A locus for familial hypertrophic cardiomyopathy is closely linked to the cardiac myosin heavy chain genes, CRI-L436, and CRI-L329 on chromosome 14 at ql 1-q- 12. *Am. J. Hum. Genet.* 47: 389–394.

Solomon, S. D., Jarcho, J. A., McKenna, W., Geisterfer-Lowrance, A. A. T., Germain, R., Salerni, R., Seidman, J. G., and Seidman, C. E. (1990b) Familial hypertrophic cardiomyopathy is a genetically heterogeneous disease. *J. Clin. Invest.* 86: 993–999.

- List those references with first authors of the same last name chronologically; however, if one or both of the authors have multiple publications, first group the publications by primary author, and then list them chronologically:

Denome, R. M., O'Callaghan, B., Luitjens, C., Harper, E., and Bianco, R. (1994) Characterization of a satellite DNA from *Antilocapra americana*. *Gene* 145 (2): 257–259.

Denome, S. A., Stanley, D. C., Olson, E. S., and Young, K. D. (1993) Metabolism of dibenzothiophene and naphthalene in *Pseudomonas* strains: complete DNA sequence of an upper naphthalene catabolic pathway. *J. Bacteriol.* 175 (21): 6890–6901.

Denome, S. A., Oldfield, C., Nash, L., and Young, K. D. (1994) Characterization of the desulfurization genes from *Rhodococcus* sp. strain IGTS8. *J. Bacteriol.* 176: 6707–6716.

Sample Student Papers in the Sciences

The following two papers were written for biology classes and follow the name-year format. The first paper, entitled "Roles of the Heat Shock Genes and Their Gene Products in *Escherichia coli*," is a literature review, and the second paper, "Determination of Protein Concentration by the Lowry Method" is a biology laboratory report. The third paper, "Oxidation of Sodium Formate/Sodium Ascorbate by Sodium Chlorite," is a simplified laboratory report from a chemistry student.

Sample Science Paper
Literature Review for Biology
Name-Year Format

Transcriptional Regulation of
Escherichia coli Heat Shock Genes
and Roles of Their Gene Products

Carol Ann Lajoie
BI 209: Microbiology
Dr. Almeida
May 1, 1990

Heat shock proteins are a class of stress proteins that have been found in every organism studied to date. Their expression in bacteria has been shown to be regulated at the transcriptional level and have a role in a wide range of processes. This paper will focus on the heat shock protein genes and gene products of the bacterium *Escherichia coli*.

When prokaryotic and eukaryotic cells are subjected to stress such as adverse environmental conditions or intracellular perturbations, a small group of proteins are synthesized (Kim *et al.,* 1987). These are referred to as stress proteins, and depending upon the stress that cells encounter, either of two classes of the proteins will be synthesized (Whelan and Hightower, 1985). The first is the glucose-regulated proteins (grps), which were originally discovered in rat and chicken embryo fibroblasts (Lee, 1987). The grps are induced by glucose starvation, glucosamine, 2deoxyglucose, tunicamycin, calcium ionophores, 2-mercaptoethanol, dithiothreitol, and low extracellular pH (Whelan and Hightower, 1985). The second class are the heat shock proteins (hsps) which are synthesized under high temperature, high external pH, amino acid analogs, sulfhydryl-reactive chemicals, and certain metal ions (Whelan and Hightower, 1985). The two most abundant hsps, hsp70 and hsp90, are highly conserved among organisms as diverse as the bacterium *E. coli,* the fruit fly *Drosophila melanogaster,* and humans, *Homo sapiens* (Pelham, Gene Products 2 1986),

---

states the topic of the paper

name and date within parentheses denote author(s) and date of publication of a source listed in literature cited

scientific names are either italicized or under-lined

Gene Products 2

perhaps suggesting that the response has its
origin in the dawn of history and is of
essential importance to cellular physiology.

The promoters of the heat shock genes have
a sequence that is distinctive from other
E. coli genes. This sequence results in the
need for an other-than-normal initiation
factor (sigma70) that will be able to
recognize the different nucleotide sequence
so that the heat shock gene products can be
synthesized. This alternative initiation
subunit is sigma32 which is encoded by the
rpo gene. The RNA polymerase binds and forms
a complex with sigma32 (as it does with
sigma70) thereby enabling it to transcribe
the heat shock genes (Johnson *et al.,* 1989).
Therefore, the initiation of the heat shock
response is regulated at the transcriptional
level.

E. coli has a set of about twenty heat
shock proteins (Pelham, 1986), and although
their method of operation is as yet
undetermined, it is believed that their
functions range from (1) association with
aberrant proteins that are the result of
stress (Kim *et al.,* 1987); (2) assembly and
disassembly of macromolecular complexes
(e.g., groE in bacteriophages T5 and T4
assembly [Fayet *et al.,* 1989]; dnaJ and dnaK
heat shock proteins in bacteriophage DNA
replication [Alfano and McMacken, 1989]); (3)
intracellular transport *(e.g.,* yeast hsp70
[Tilly *et al.,* 1989]); (4) transcription
(e.g., sigma70 and GroE [Tilly *et al.,* 1989]);
(5) proteolysis *(e.g.,* Lon [Tilly *et al.,*

1989]); and (6) translation (*e.g.*, lys1-tRNA synthetase [Tilly *et al.*, 1989]). The protein of a particular heat shock gene is considered to be indispensable (*e.g.*, rpoD, which codes for the sigma70 subunit of *E. coli* RNA polymerase), dispensable (*e.g.*, lysU, which codes for an alternate form of lys1-tRNA synthetase), or conditionally dispensable (*e.g.*, dnaK and dnaJ) meaning that deletion mutants can be created at low temperatures but they replicate poorly and quickly amass extragenic suppressers (Fayet *et al.*, 1989).

The groE operon consists of two genes, groES and groEL. Their gene products are acidic polypeptides with molecular weights of 10,368 and 57,259 Da., respectively. They are intracellular and at normal growth temperature (37°C) comprise a sizable portion (approximately 2%) of the cellular proteins. These proteins belong to the heat shock regulon. Fayet *et al.* (1989) demonstrated that when *E. coli* are shifted from 37°C to a higher but nonlethal temperature their synthesis is increased. Transduction experiments have shown the need for groE gene products at low as well as high temperatures. The groE gene products also have a role in the assembly of macromolecular complexes (Tilly *et al.*, 1989). A morphogenetic role for groE gene products has been reported. In conjunction with each other, groES and groEL gene products are necessary for the prohead assembly of bacteriophage Lambda (Tilly *et al.*, 1981) and phage T5 tail assembly (Zweig and Cummings, 1973), while the groEL gene

Gene Products 4

product alone is required for phage T4 head assembly (Revel *et al.*, 1980).

E. coli rpoH deletion mutants have demonstrated the importance of the groE genes in the heat shock response. The rpoH parent was temperature sensitive and not capable of growth at temperatures higher than 20°C whereas temperature-resistant revertants of an rpoH mutant were viable at temperatures as high as 40°C. It was demonstrated that the temperature resistant revertants had obtained an insertion upstream of the groE genes, which resulted in a sigma70-dependent increase in the levels of groE gene products. This coincides with a sigma70-dependent promoter that is located twenty-five to thirty bases downstream of the sigma32-dependent promoter in the groE operon (Fayet *et al.*, 1989).

Hemmingsen *et al.* (1988) determined that the amino acid sequence of the groEL gene product of *E. coli* is 46% identical to the rubisco subunit-binding protein of plant chloroplasts. In addition, McMullin and Hallenberg (1987, 1988) showed that groEL is related to the hsp58 gene product that is localized after heat shock in mitochondria. This evidence seems to demonstrate an apparent conservation of the groE gene over time.

The bacterial heat shock protein equivalent to the eukaryotic hsp70 protein is the dnaK protein (Ang and Georgopoulos, 1989). There is sufficient genetic and biochemical data supporting a direct, physical interaction

between the grpE and dnaK gene products
(Johnson *et al.*, 1989). The dnaK protein
apparently operates in protein stabilization,
refolding, and dissociation (Johnson *et al.*,
1989). It, along with another heat shock
protein, dnaJ, is essential in Lambda DNA
replication (Ang and Georgopoulos, 1989;
Johnson *et al.*, 1989). Sakakibara (1988) has
shown that dnaK, dnaJ, and grpE proteins are
required for *E. coli* replication. The role of
these proteins in *E. coli* replication may be
similar to their role in initiation of Lambda
DNA replication. Hydrophobic interactions
between the Lambda P and bacterial dnaK
proteins initiate a series of events leading
to DNA replication by disrupting the Lambda
P-dnaB complex (Johnson *et al.*, 1989).

The dnaK gene product is a negative
regulator of the heat shock response (Tilly
et al., 1983). Proteins that are susceptible
to the heat shock response are denatured
causing hydrophobic areas of the polypeptide
to be exposed. This has been shown to be a
eukaryotic heat shock response inducing signal
(Ananthan *et al.*, 1986). The dnaK protein
possibly functions in the stabilization or
refolding of heat-denatured proteins by
protecting the exposed hydrophobic regions
(Ang and Georgopoulos, 1989). This would
eliminate the inducing signal. As for the
dnaJ and grpE genes, their exact role in the
heat shock response is uncertain. It may be
that they work with and aid the dnaK protein
in controlling the heat shock response (Ang
and Georgopoulos, 1989).

Gene Products 6

*views
ajor points
the paper*

In summary, heat shock proteins are a ubiquitous class of stress proteins with distinctive promoters requiring a unique RNA polymerase initiation factor. The hsps function in a wide range of processes. For example, the groE gene product is required for bacterial growth at both high and low temperatures and has a role in the assembly of bacteriophages Lambda, T4, and T5. The bacterial dnaK protein, which is related to the eukaryotic hsp70 family of proteins, is a negative regulator of the heat shock response and possibly mediates protein stabilization, refolding, and dissociation. In addition, the dnaK protein has a possible role in the replication of *E. coli* and Lambda DNA when in association with the dnaJ proteins and the dnaJ and grpE proteins, respectively.

Literature Cited

sources listed alphabetically

Alfano, C., and McMacken, R. (1989) Heat shock protein-mediated disassembly of nucleoprotein structures is required for the initiation of bacteriophage Lambda DNA replication. *J. Biol. Chem.* 264 (18): 10709-10718.

first letter of first word of the title is capitalized

Ananthan, J., Goldberg, A. L., and Voellmy, R. (1986) Abnormal proteins serve as eukaryotic stress signals and trigger the activation of heat shock genes. *Science* 232: 522-524.

Ang, D., and Georgopoulos, C. (1989) The heat-shock-regulated grpE gene of *Escherichia coli is* required for bacterial growth at all temperatures but is dispensable in certain mutant backgrounds. *J. Bact.* 171 (5): 2748-2755.

journal's name is abbreviated

Fayet, O., Ziegelhoffer, T., and Georgopoulos, C. (1989) The groES and groEL heat shock gene products of *Escherichia coli* are essential for bacterial growth at all temperatures. *J. Bact.* 171 (3): 1379-1385.

Hemmingsen, S. M., Woolford, C., van der Vies, S. M., Tilly, K., Dennis, D. T., Georgopoulos, C. P., Hendrix, R. W., and Ellis, R. J. (1988) Homologous plant and bacterial proteins chaperone oligomeric protein assembly. *Nature* (London) 333: 330-334.

Gene Products 8

Johnson, C., Chandrasekhar, G. N., and
Georgopoulos C. (1989) *Escherichia coli* dnaK
and grpE heat shock proteins interact both *in
vivo* and *in vitro*. *J. Bact.* 171 (3):
1590-1596.

Kim, Y. K., Kim, K. S., and Lee, A. S. (1987)
Regulation of the glucose-regulated protein
genes by ß-mercaptoethanol requires *de novo*
protein synthesis and correlates with
inhibition of protein glycosylation. *J. Cell.
Phys.* 133: 553-559.

Lee, A. S. (1987) Coordinated regulation of a
set of genes by glucose and calcium
ionophores in mammalian cells. *Trends Biol.
Scien.* 12 (1): 20-23.

McMullin, T. W., and Hallberg, R. L. (1987) A
normal mitochondrial protein is selectively
synthesized and accumulated during heat shock
in *Tetrahymena thermophila*. *Mol. Cell Biol.*
7: 4414-4423.

McMullin, T. W., and Hallenberg, R. L. (1988)
A highly evolutionarily conserved
mitochondrial protein is structurally related
to protein encoded by the *Escherichia coli*
groEL gene. *Mol. Cell. Biol.* 8: 371-380.

Pelham, H.R.B. (1986) Speculations on the
functions of the major heat shock and
glucose-regulated proteins. *Cell* 46: 959-961.

Revel, H. R., Stitt, B. R., Lielausis, I., and Wood, W. B. (1980) Role of the host cell in bacteriophage T4 development. 1. Characterization of host mutants that block T4 head assembly. *J. Virol.* 33: 366-376.

Sakakibara, Y. (1988) The dnaK gene of *Escherichia coli* functions in initiation of chromosome replication. *J. Bact.* 170 (2): 972-979.

Tilly K., Murialdo, H., and Georgopoulos, C. (1981) Identification of a second *E. coli* groE gene whose product is necessary for bacteriophage morphogenesis. *Proc. Nat. Acad. Scien. U.S.A.* 78: 1629-1633.

Tilly, K., McKittrick, N., Zylicz, M., and Georgopoulos, C. (1983) The dnaK protein modulates the heat shock response of *Escherichia coli*. *Cell* 34: 641-646.

Tilly, K., Spence, J., and Georgopoulos, C. (1989) Modulation of stability of the *Escherichia coli* heat shock regulatory factor sigma 32. *J. Bact.* 171 (3): 1585-1589.

Whelan, S. A., and Hightower, L. E. (1985) Differential induction of glucose-regulated and heat shock proteins: effects of pH and sulfhydryl-reducing agents on chicken embryo cells. *J. Cell. Phys.* 125: 251-258.

Zweig, M., and Cummings, D. J. (1973) Cleavage of head and tail proteins during bacteriophage T5 assembly: selective host involvement in the cleavage of a tail protein. *J. Mol. Biol.* 80: 505-518.

Sample Science Paper
Laboratory Report for Biology
Name-Year Format

Protein Quantification by
the Lowry Method

Joseph Coleman
BI 415: Cellular Biochemistry
Dr. Almeida
May 1, 1990

Abstract

concisely states the purpose, method and conclusion of the study

The Lowry method is an accurate means of determining protein concentration within the range of 10-300 $\mu g/mL$. The principle entails two separate reactions. The first is the binding of copper ions (CU2+) in a dilute alkaline copper sulfate solution complex to nitrogen atoms within the peptide bonds of protein, producing a pink to violet colored complex. Subsequently the Folin-Ciocalteu phenol reagent binds to tyrosine and tryptophan residues within the protein, producing a blue-green coloration. The quantity of protein in the sample is determined by measuring the color intensity, using a spectrophotometer. The Lowry method was used in this study to determine the concentration of protein within rabbit skeletal and pig heart muscle samples.

Introduction

justfication and applicability of the technique used in the study

Molecular biologists often have a need to determine the presence of and/or quantify protein in a sample. The effectiveness of these techniques is limited due to a narrow sensitivity range or are dependent upon the concentration of particular amino acids within the protein. Therefore, a method is needed to detect small quantities of a wide range of proteins accurately and quickly. The Lowry (1951) method used in this study for protein quantification is based on two earlier techniques, the biuret assay and the Folin-Ciocalteu reaction.

Protein Quantification 1

The biuret assay relies on the interaction between copper ions ($CU2+$) and the amide nitrogen atom within the peptide bond between amino acids. Because this complex produces a purple color, the intensity of the color indicates the amount of the protein present in the sample. The inadequacies of the biuret assay are its insensitivity to low protein concentrations and its inaccuracy in the presence of Tris (Robson *et al.*, 1968), ammonia (Gornall *et al.*, 1949) and glycerol (Zishka and Nishimura, 1970).

relevant background information

Lowry *et al.*, (1951) modified the biuret assay, making it more than 100 times more sensitive by introducing the Folin-Ciocalteu (1927) phenol reagent. The Folin-Ciocalteu phenol reagent contains phosphomolybdate and phosphotungstate which oxidizes tyrosine and tryptophan side chains, resulting in blue-green coloration. Although the Lowry method has increased sensitivity compared to the biuret assay, it has an inherent disadvantage—the tyrosine and tryptophan concentration is being measured and not necessarily the concentration of the proteins in the sample since the quantity of tyrosine and tryptophan can vary among proteins. Therefore, the Lowry method is best used for monitoring the change in, and not the precise values of, protein concentration and is only valid when the proteins have uniform tyrosine and tryptophan contents. In addition, the relationship between color development and protein content is linear over the range of 10-300 μg protein per mL of solvent (Lowry *et al.*, 1951).

name and date within parentheses denote author(s) and date of publication of a source listed in literature cited

Protein Quantification 1

The amount of color production is determined using a spectrophotometer, which measures the amount of light absorbed by a substance. In the Lowry assay the amount of light absorbed is proportional to the quantity of protein in the sample being tested. The amount of protein within a sample can be determined by comparing it with a set of standards containing known protein concentrations. A standard curve is constructed by plotting the absorbance (*i.e.,* optical density) on the *y*-axis and protein concentration on the *x*-axis. Using the optical density of an unknown can be used to interpolate the protein content of the sample.

purpose of the study restated

This study focuses on the quantification of protein in two samples: rabbit skeletal and pig heart muscle. Both samples were homogenized and diluted and had their optical densities recorded. A standard curve constructed using lysozyme, which has a uniform tyrosine and tryptophan content, was used to interpolate the concentration of the muscle protein samples.

Protein Quantification 2

Materials and Methods

A set of protein standards was created using a 1.0 mg/mL stock solution. The lysozyme solution was diluted as directed in Table 1, with a final volume of 1.2 mL in each tube.

title placed above the table

Table 1: Preparation of Lysozyme Standards

Tube #	Lysozyme stock volume (mL)	Water volume (mL)
1	0.00	1.20
2	0.06	1.14
3	0.12	1.08
4	0.18	1.02
5	0.24	0.96
6	0.48	0.72
7	0.60	0.60
8	0.90	0.30

Rabbit skeletal and pig heart muscle protein extracts were prepared using 4 g of each tissue. The muscle was minced into very small pieces and then homogenized in 16 mL of 50 nM potassium phosphate buffer, pH 7.0, 4°C (4.1 g KH_2PO_4/L; 3.5 g K_2HPO_4/L). The extract was then centrifuged for 10 min. at 10,000 r.p.m. in a Sorvall centrifuge. A glass wool plugged funnel was used to filter the decanted supernatant. This stock solution containing crude protein extract was diluted 10-fold by adding 18 mL of 50 mM potassium phosphate buffer, pH 7.0, 4°C to 2 mL of the extract. The protein extract was diluted further as directed in Table 2, with a final volume of 1.2 mL in each tube.

procedure for preparation of muscle extracts

Table 2: Preparation of Muscle Extract Dilutions		
Tube #	Protein volume (mL)	Water volume (mL)
9	1.20 heart muscle supernatant	0.00
10	0.60 heart muscle supernatant	0.60
11	0.30 heart muscle supernatant	0.90
12	0.12 heart muscle supernatant	1.08
13	0.06 heart muscle supernatant	1.14
14	0.03 heart muscle supernatant	1.17
15	0.01 heart muscle supernatant	1.19
16	1.20 skeletal muscle supernatant	0.00
17	0.60 skeletal muscle supernatant	0.60
18	0.30 skeletal muscle supernatant	0.90
19	0.12 skeletal muscle supernatant	1.08
20	0.06 skeletal muscle supernatant	1.14
21	0.03 skeletal muscle supernatant	1.17
22	0.01 skeletal muscle supernatant	1.19

previously described methods is referenced

The copper sulfate reagent was prepared by combining 2 mL of 1% $CUSO_4$-$5H_2O$; 2 mL of 2% sodium potassium tartrate; 196 mL of 2% Na_2CO_3 in 0.1 M NaOH. The Folin reagent was prepared as previously described (Folin and Ciocalteu, 1927).

assay procedure

The Lowry assay was carried out by adding 6 mL of the copper sulfate solution to each tube, mixing well and incubating at room temperature for 10 minutes. Each tube then received 0.3 mL of 1N Folin reagent, mixed, and incubated at room temperature for 30 minutes. The absorbance of each tube was recorded at 500 nm after the spectrophotometer was zeroed using tube #1.

Protein Quantification 4

The concentration of lysozyme in each of the standard tubes was calculated by multiplying its respective dilution factor by the concentration of the stock tube. The absorbences and protein concentrations for the standards were plotted, and the best fit line was drawn. The absorbences of the muscle extracts which correspond to the linear portion of the curve were used to interpolate the sample tubes' diluted protein content. The amount of protein in the original protein sample was determined by multiplying the diluted protein concentration of a tube by its total dilution factor. The protein concentration in each of the stock tubes containing the crude protein extract was determined by calculating the mean of the stock protein concentrations.

graph construction and inter-polation

Results

The optical density values at 500 nm (O.D.$_{500}$) for each of the tubes are represented in column 2 of Table 3. Also represented in Table 3 are the lysozyme concentrations used as standards (column 3), the diluted protein concentrations interpolated from the graph for the sample tubes having absorbences corresponding to the linear portion of the curve (column 4); and the concentration of the heart and skeletal muscle stock solutions (column 5).

giving specific locations adds clarity and focuses reader's attention

Protein Quantification 5

Table 3: Lowry Assay Data

Tube #	O. D._500	[Lysozyme] (mg/mL)	Diluted [Protein] (mg/mL)	Original [Protein] (mg/mL)
1	0.00	0.00	----	----
2	0.06	0.05	----	----
3	0.121	0.10	----	----
4	0.178	0.15	----	----
5	0.242	0.20	----	----
6	0.315	0.30	----	----
7	0.388	0.40	----	----
8	0.421	0.50	----	----
9	0.730	----	----	----
10	0.479	----	----	----
11	0.274	----	----	----
12	0.125	----	0.108	10.8
13	0.056	----	0.048	9.6
14	0.046	----	0.037	14.8
15	0.018	----	0.013	15.6
16	0.850	----	----	----
17	0.484	----	----	----
18	0.311	----	----	----
19	3.142	----	0.122	12.2
20	0.073	----	0.058	11.6
21	0.050	----	0.040	16.0
22	0.021	----	0.017	20.4

results are stated without analysis

The graph in Figure 1 shows a best fit line drawn using the absorbences and lysozyme concentrations for the first eight (standard) tubes. The mean of the original protein concentration values calculated for the pig heart and rabbit skeletal muscles are 12.7 mg/mL and 15.1 mg/mL, respectively.

Protein Quantification 6

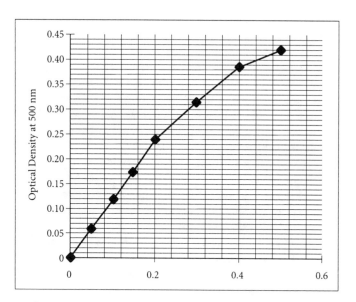

Figure 1: Standard Curve for Lowry Assay.
Plot of optical density at 500 nm versus
lysozyme concentration within each of the
standard samples.

title and
legend are
below illus-
tration

Discussion

The Lowry assay is sensitive within the
range of 0.01-0.3 mg/mL of protein (Lowry *et
al.*, 1951). This was demonstrated in the lab
by the nonlinearity of the standard curve
above 0.25 mg/mL, indicating our experimental
results are very close to the norm. The last
four and most dilute protein concentrations
that were interpolated from the standard
curve can be considered the most accurate due
to the sensitivity of the Lowry assay and the
nonlinearity of the standard curve beyond

analysis of
results

0.25 mg/mL. The remaining values approach or exceed the range of the Lowry assay. The mean of the original protein concentrations is believed to represent the concentrations of protein in the original crude protein extracts. The protein concentration from the heart tissue extract is 12.7 mg/mL, while the concentration of protein in the skeletal tissue extract is 15.1 mg/mL.

explanation of variation in data

Different dilutions of the protein samples did not yield the same original protein concentration and this may be due to factors inherent to the Lowry assay that are hard to circumvent. Since the Lowry assay is sensitive to a small protein concentration, then assays which contain too high a protein concentration would be off the standard curve and not be able to give consistent or reliable results. On the other hand, assays with low protein concentrations require pipetting very small amounts which bring into question the reliability of the volumes transferred into the assayed tube. Keeping these factors in mind, it seems reasonable to assume that more than one set of assay values would be needed to determine an accurate protein concentration.

Acknowledgments

I would like to thank Prof. Almeida for his assistance during the lab, and also the Lajoie Farm for providing the muscle tissues analyzed.

Protein Quantification 5

Literature Cited

Folin, O., and Ciocalteu, V. (1927) On tyrosine and tryptophane determinations in proteins. *J. Biol. Chem.* 73: 627.

Gornall, A. G., Bardawill, C. J., and David, M. M. (1949) Determination of serum proteins by means of the biuret reaction. *J. Biol. Chem.* 177: 751-766.

Lowry, O. H., Rosebrough, N. J., Farr, A. L., and Randall, R. J. (1951) Protein measurement with the folin, phenol reagent. *J. Biol. Chem* 193: 265-275.

Robson, R. M., Goll, D. E., and Temple, M. J. (1968) Determination of proteins in "Tris" buffer by the biuret reaction. *Anal. Biochem.* 24 (2): 339-341.

Zishka, M. K., and Nishimura, J. S. (1970) Effect of glycerol on Lowry and biuret methods of protein determination. *Anal. Biochem.* 34: 291-297.

Sample Science Paper
Simplified Laboratory Report
for Chemistry

INSTRUMENTAL ANALYSIS LABORATORY REPORT

Oxidation of Sodium Formate/Sodium
Ascorbate by Sodium Chlorite
by
Pamela J. Kelly

CH332
Professor Maria A. Curtin

Oxidation 1

Abstract: The oxidation of sodium ascorbate by sodium chlorite is a highly exothermic reaction. In theory the reaction of sodium formate with sodium chlorite is also highly exothermic and produces carbon dioxide. Because these reactions give off large amounts of heat, they could possibly be used by soldiers in the field in place of the Flameless Ration Heaters (FRH). Flameless Ration Heaters (FRH) are carried by soldiers to heat up their meal-ready-to-eat. The current FRH has a major disadvantage in that it produces hydrogen gas, an extremely flammable gas. Product analysis of the reaction of a mixture of sodium formate and sodium ascorbate with sodium chlorite gave 78.63% of the sodium chlorite going to chloride ions. Oxalate ions were also found as a product of the reaction.

Introduction

In this section, we set out to study the oxidation of a mixture of sodium ascorbate and sodium formate by the strong oxidizing agent sodium chlorite. Focus will be placed on the quantitative analysis of the products that we get. We will answer questions such as, did the reaction go to completion, were our methods accurate enough, and what errors occurred? The oxidation of formate produces carbon dioxide; however, this reaction does not occur spontaneously. This is where sodium ascorbate comes into play because it readily reacts with the oxidizing agent and could be used to initiate the formate/chlorite

Oxidation 2

reaction. Since these reactions are oxidation-reduction reactions, we can look at their half reactions. The oxidation of sodium formate produces carbon dioxide.

$$HCO_2 = CO_2 + H^+ + 2e^-$$

The oxidation of sodium ascorbate produces dehydroascorbic acid.

$$C_6O_6H_7 = C_6O_6H_6 + H^+ + 2e^-$$

The reaction of sodium chlorite produces chloride ions.

$$ClO_2 + 2H_2O + 4e^- = Cl^- + 4OH^-$$

The half reactions of sodium formate or sodium ascorbate are multiplied by a factor of two so they can be coupled with that of sodium chlorite. In this way the number of electrons produced by the oxidation is equal to those needed for the reduction. The resulting reactions are as follows:

$$ClO_2^- + 2H_2O + 2C_6O_6H_7^- = Cl^- + 4OH^- + 2C_6O_6H_6 + 2H^+$$

$$2HCO_2^- + ClO_2^- + 2H_2O = Cl^- + 4OH^- + 2CO_2 + 2H^+$$

Experimental Design and Procedures

Reagents

Sodium chlorite, technical grade (Aldrich)	$KMnO_4$ (Fisher)
Sodium formate (Fisher Scientific)	Sodium oxalate (Thom Smith)
Sodium ascorbate (Aldrich)	$Ca(NO_3)_2$ (Fisher Scientific)
HCl (Fisher Scientific)	Ammonium hydroxide, concentrated (Fisher)
Na_2CO_3 (Fisher)	Deionized water
$AgNO_3$ (Fisher)	Dichlorofluorescein indicator (Fisher)
Dextrin (Fisher)	H_2SO_4 concentrated (Fisher)

Reaction I: First, we dissolved 0.061 moles of sodium chlorite, 0.102 moles of sodium formate and 0.010 moles of buffer (Na_2CO_3) in 50 mL of water. (The basic buffer is necessary to prevent decomposition of the chlorite ion in solution.) To this solution, we added 0.027 moles of sodium ascorbate and allowed it to react. After about 10 minutes the reaction mixture began to change color and CO_2 was evolved. The reaction was stirred with a magnetic stirrer and was complete in about 15 minutes to give a pale yellow solution.

Chloride ion determinations: The amount of chloride ion produced by the oxidation of sodium formate and sodium ascorbate by sodium chlorite was determined using Fajan's method.

Preparation of solutions:
A silver nitrate solution (0.0100 M) was prepared by dissolving 8.5004 g of $AgNO_3$ in boiled distilled water.

A dextrin solution, a solution used to prevent the coagulation of the AgCl, was prepared by dissolving 0.01 g of dextrin in 100 mL of distilled water.

Chloride Titration: Fajan's method:
(Note: To ensure safety, all sample treatments and titrations were carried out under the hood.) A blank solution of sodium chlorite (0.061 moles) and the Na_2CO_3 buffer (0.010 moles) in water was titrated first. A 25 mL aliquot of the blank solution was placed in a 250 mL Erlenmeyer flask. It was

Oxidation 4

acidified dropwise with concentrated H_2SO_4
to a pH between 6 and 7. (This step was
performed to prevent the precipitation of
the silver as silver carbonate or silver
hydroxide, both of which are insoluble in
water. Acidifying the solution does cause
some decomposition of the sodium chlorite, so
all experimental procedures should be carried
out under the hood to avoid any chlorine
fumes.) Ten milliliters of the dextrin
solution were added to our acidified blank
along with several drops of dichlorofluoro-
escein. Quickly and soon after acidification,
the titration with our $AgNO_3$ (0.1 M) was
performed. This titration with the blank
solution was carried out with two more 25 mL
aliquots. All of the results were recorded.
Next, we had to run our basic reaction
(Reaction 1) as described earlier. The
resulting solution was transferred
quantitatively to a volumetric flask and
diluted to 500 mL. For our titration, we took
a 25 mL aliquot of the diluted solution and
placed it in a 250 Erlenmeyer flask. It was
acidified as in the procedure above. Ten
milliliters of dextrin and a few drops of
dichlorofluorocein were added to it. It was
then titrated with the silver nitrate in the
hood. This titration was carried out with two
more 25 mL aliquots. All of the results were
recorded. From our numbers, we calculated the
amount of chloride ion produced in the basic
reaction.

<u>Oxalate determination</u>:

Although oxalate ions do not show up in the reaction schemes for the oxidation of formate and ascorbate by sodium chlorite, the possibility of the production of oxalate ions exists either from the further oxidation of sodium ascorbate or the combination of intermediates during the reaction. The determination of oxalate was carried out by titrating the oxalate with potassium permanganate.

Preparation of solutions:

$KMnO4$ standard solution was prepared by dissolving 3.201 g $KMnO4$ in one liter of water and heating it for an hour just below boiling. It was covered and left to stand until the next lab period. Then, the solution was filtered through a fine porosity filter and placed in a clean amber glass bottle.

A calcium solution was prepared by taking 12.045 g of $Ca(NO_3)_2$ dissolved in distilled water and diluting to 250 mL in a volumetric flask.

Permanganate standardization titration:

Three samples of sodium oxalate were weighed out (~0.100 g each) and dissolved in 250 mL of H_2SO_4 (3M), each in separate 500 mL Erlenmeyer flasks. Each of the three solutions was titrated with the $KMnO_4$ using a 50 mL buret. With each titration, between 5 to 10 mL of $KMnO_4$ solution was added to the oxalate sample quickly. After the color disappeared, the solution was heated with a hot plate to 55-60°C. The titration was

Oxidation 6

completed at this temperature. All three
titration results were recorded. A blank
solution of 300 mL of sulfuric acid was also
titrated with the $KMnO_4$ solution until the
color matched that of the titrated oxalate
samples. (The volume of $KMnO_4$ required to
titrate the blank was subtracted from the
final volumes of the standards.) With all of
the numbers recorded, calculations were done
to determine the exact molarity of the $KMnO_4$
solution.

*Determination of oxalate produced by the
formate/ascorbate oxidation:*
  Our oxidation/reduction reaction was
carried out as described earlier (reaction 1)
and diluted to 500 mL in a volumetric flask.
A 10.00 mL aliquot of the diluted solution
was transferred to a 250 mL Erlenmeyer flask.
Then 10.00 mL of the calcium solution were
added to the flask. The pH of the solution
was checked using a pH meter (Corning). It
was brought to a pH between 8-10, using
ammonium hydroxide. The solution was stirred
for about fifteen minutes with a magnetic
stirrer. A precipitate formed, indicating
oxalate was present. The precipitate was
filtered through a fine porosity filter
crucible. The precipitate was washed with hot
distilled water. The crucible and its
contents (precipitate) were transferred to a
600 mL beaker. Two hundred mL of hot H_2SO_4
(3M) were added to this solution and it was
heated to 85°C with a hot plate. The sample
was then titrated with the standardized $KMnO_4$

Oxidation 7

until a faint pink color lasted for at least
30 seconds. The temperature of the solution
was kept above 60°C for the whole titration.
The procedure was performed with two more
aliquots of our sample. All of the results
were recorded. By using the molarity of the
potassium permanganate previously calculated,
we were able to calculate the amount of
oxalate produced in our original reaction.

Results and Discussion

Table 1: Amounts of reactants used in reaction	
Chemical	Amount
Sodium chlorite	5.492 g
Sodium formate	6.846 g
Sodium carbonate (buffer)	1.150 g
Sodium ascorbate	5.348 g
Deionized water	50 mL

Reaction I

Titration for chloride ion determination.
This step was performed to determine
the amount of chloride ion produced from the
sodium chlorite reaction. A blank titration
was done because the sodium chlorite is 80%
technical grade and is very likely to have
some Cl^- present.

Table 2: Blank titration			
Blank	Volume (initial), mL	Volume (final), mL	Endpoint, mL
I	No good	------	------
2	0.10	6.22	6.12
3	6.22	14.40	8.18
Average blank = 7.15 mL			

Flask	Volume (initial), mL	Volume (final), mL	Endpoint	Amount of Cl^- (moles)	Percent Cl produced
		Table 3: Chloride determination			
1	0.50	31.45	23.80	0.0476	78.03
2	0.0	31.20	24.05	0.0481	78.85
3	0.10	31.35	24.10	0.0482	79.02

8.5004 g $AgNO_3$/169.8717g/mol =
0.05004 mol/0.5 L = 0.1000 M = Molarity of $AgNO_3$

(Molarity of Titrant)(Volume of Titrant) = (Molarity Unknown)(Volume of Unknown)

Average endpoint = endpoint - blank = 31.25 - 7.15 = 24.10 mL

(0.1000M)(0.2310 L) = moles Cl^-

moles of Cl^- produced by reaction = moles Cl^- X(500/25) = 0.0482 mol

(actual)/(theoretical) x 100 = percent yield

(0.0482 mol)/(0.061 mol) x 100 = 79.02%

average percent = 78.63 %

Discussion of chloride determinations:
   Several errors could have occurred so that we would not have recovered all of our chloride ions. The first thing that could have happened deals with the blank. Our first run with the blank was no good, and the other two endpoints were close, but they were not as close as we would like them to be. Since the procedure calls for the titrations to be carried out quickly after acidification, time

Oxidation 9

could have definitely been a factor. The
reaction could have decomposed if it had been
allowed to sit too long before titration.
Also, the end point could have been passed or
not even reached for that matter. The color
change was not a sharp one, making it
extremely difficult to judge the endpoint.
Other determinate errors could have affected
the titration. Factors like miscalculation
when making solutions could have occurred.
Overall, the numbers were fairly consistent
with each other.

Oxalate determination

Permanganate standardization

Table 4: Pennanganate standardization			
Flask #	Endpoint	Oxalate weight (g)	Molarity
1	15.20	0.1010	0.01984
2	16.25	0.1100	0.02022
3	14.45	0.1010	0.02087

Average Molarity Permanganate = 0.02031

oxalate weight/133.948g/mol = moles oxalate

moles oxalate = M permanganate (0.01520 L)5/2
= 0.019843 M

Determination of oxalate:

This step was performed to find the amount
of oxalate produced from our reaction. The
molarity of the permanganate solution
calculated above was used in the
determination.

Oxidation 10

Table 5: Oxalate Determination			
Flask#	Endpoint (mL)	Blank (mL) (moles)	Amount of oxalate	Percent oxalate
1	9.55	0.02	0.02419	89.6
2	9.3	0.02	0.02356	87.3
3	9.65	0.02	0.02444	90.5

moles oxalate = Molarity of titrant x Volume of Titrant x (5/2)(0.02031 M)(0.00955 - 0.00002 L)(5/2)(500/10) = moles oxalate in reaction = 0.02419

actual/theoretical x 100 = percent yield 0.02419/0.027 moles x 100 = 89.6%

average percent = 89.1%

Discussion of oxalate determination:

  The theoretical amount of oxalate was defined as the number of moles of sodiurn ascorbate in the reaction. It was assurned that the oxalate was produced by the further oxidation of the ascorbate in a one to one ratio. Some of the sources of error were as follows: Obviously, the molarity is not totally exact because the endpoint is a range. We could have passed the endpoint slightly. If the standardization and calculation of the molarity of permanganate were incorrect, this would make the calculation of the amount of oxalate produced incorrect as well.

Conclusion

In the determination of chloride ions produced by our reaction of sodium formate, sodium ascorbate, and sodium chlorite, our calculated results were very consistent. Our numbers were approximately seventy-eight percent for each of the three trials. This result indicates that all of the chlorite is converted to chloride. However, although we determined a fairly high percent yield, certain aspects could still be improved to get a more accurate and precise result. We would suggest working on this section again, this time making even more careful measurements and calculations than in our previous experiment.

In the determination of the oxalate ions produced by our reaction, once again, our calculated results were fairly consistent. The numbers that were determined were approximately eighty-nine percent for each of the three trials. This indicates that the ascorbate is probably further oxidized to give oxalate. Although the mechanism of the reaction is not the subject of this report, we must wonder as to where exactly the oxalate comes from and by what mechanism. The experimental determination of the amount of oxalate produced, we feel, worked extremely well. Precision was good.

Overall, this entire lab, Section I and Section II, was a learning experience. It was very interesting to perform lab experiments as if we were in a research lab. Hopefully, the

Oxidation 12

methods used in both can be improved upon
using the knowledge gained from our
experiments this semester.

References

Christian, G. D. (1994) *Analytical chemistry.*
5th ed. New York, NY: John Wiley & Sons, Inc.

Curtin, M. A. (1997) *Analytical chemistry
laboratory manual,* 3rd ed. Stonehill College,
Easton, MA.

Hargis, L. G. (1988) *Analytical chemistry:
principles and techniques.* Upper Saddle River,
NJ: Prentice Hall.

Harris, D. C. (1995) *Quantitative chemical
analysis,* 4th ed. New York, NY: W. H. Freeman
& Company.

WRITING IN BUSINESS

Business writing involves correspondence and reports. Its primary purpose is to inform business associates, vendors, customers, and other interested parties of what is being or has been done, or to persuade them to do something. Various types of business correspondence and reports follow specific prescribed formats. The text within these formats may develop inductively or deductively, depending on the purpose of the document.

Research Sources

Information for reports may come from either primary or secondary sources. Primary research can be conducted to determine what resources are available, what other businesses are doing, or what changes are occurring in the marketplace. This research may take the form of interviews, surveys, observation, or analysis of internal records. Library searches can be utilized to help find secondary data on specific companies and competition, market and industry information, economic conditions, political and legal conditions, changing demographics, technology, and global issues or historical events that may affect business operations.

The resources available for library searches are extensive. Some are available in print, on CD-ROM (compact disk—read only memory), and on-line.

Specialized Library Sources

The references listed will give the business student some resources with which to start. They are appropriate for students studying accounting, computer information systems, finance, management, marketing, and other areas of business. The following will provide useful information about companies, markets, economic conditions, and other important business factors. The specific reference sources listed represent only a fraction of what is available. Each library is unique in its offerings, so it is best to consult the reference librarian at your particular library to find out what is available.

Periodical and Newspaper Indexes

Indexes can be used as guides to locate relevant information found in a variety of publications and other sources. Proper use of indexes can reduce the amount of time needed to find the required information. Current information on a variety of business topics can be located by using indexes like those listed below.

Business Periodicals Index
New York Times Index
Reader's Guide to Periodical Literature
Social Sciences Index
Wall Street Journal Index

Many indexes are also available on CD-ROM. Cited journals may also be tagged to indicate the library's holdings.

If you cannot find the journal or newspaper to which one of these indexes refers you, you should see the reference librarian. Most academic libraries participate in interlibrary loan and can obtain materials from other libraries.

Specialized Databases for Computer Searches

As mentioned, many periodical and newspaper indexes can also be accessed through the use of CD-ROM workstations. Many other important databases can be accessed through CD-ROM as well, and some examples are listed below.

ABI/Inform
Compact Disclosure
National Trade Data Bank
Wilson Business Abstracts

Check with the reference librarian for the databases that are available on CD-ROM at your library. Certain databases are also available on-line.

On-Line Services

Most libraries have computers where one can access information found on the Internet. Internet users have access to a wide variety of information. Most companies have their own Web sites and can provide a wealth of information. Many government agencies, such as the IRS, also have their own Web sites with useful information.

A library's computerized literature search service is another useful research tool. This on-line service provides access to individual databases. This service allows you to do the equivalent of a periodical index search on your research topic by providing access to the databases of vendors such as Dialog, STN, and Nexis. See the reference librarian for assistance on computerized literature searches.

Economic Indicators

Certain periodicals provide information on leading economic indicators. The *Survey of Current Business* is a good source for information on economic indicators.

U.S. Government and Private Publications

The following publications yield valuable demographic and statistical information.

> *Business Statistics*
> *Dun and Bradstreet's Industry Norm and Key Business Ratios*
> *Economic Censuses*
> *Moody's Industry Review*
> *Standard and Poor's Industry Surveys*

Some of the sources listed may also be available on-line. Two useful internet sites for access to statistical information are the SEC EDGAR Database (http://www.ec.gov:80/edgarhp.htm) and FED-STATS: A TO Z (http://www.fedstats.gov/). Be aware that Web site addresses are subject to change.

Corporate Annual Reports

Current reports for many corporations are available on CD-ROM, on-line, and on microfiche in libraries. *Compact Disclosure* available through CD-ROM provides access to annual reports. *Annual Reports Online* (http://zpub.com/sf/arl/arl-www.html) provides information and guidance on how to access annual reports on the Internet. Reports can also be obtained directly from the company's headquarters.

Directories and Registers

Corporate addresses and basic operating information can be obtained from directories and registers. The following represents examples of these.

> *Dun and Bradstreet's Million Dollar Directory*
> *Macmillan Directory of Leading Private Companies*
> *Moody's Manuals*
> *Standard and Poor's Register of Corporations*
> *Thomas Register on American Manufacturers*

Nonlibrary Sources

Much research for business is conducted by sorting through company records; interviewing, questioning, and surveying appropriate people; observing performance and production; and writing to various government departments and bureaus. Some of these are the U.S. Bureau of Industrial Economics, the Industry Publications Division, Trade Development, the U.S. Bureau of Census, and the U.S. Department of Commerce. Company annual reports can usually be obtained by writing directly to the company, and additional information can be obtained about a small company by writing to or calling local newspapers in the town in which the company is located.

Assignments in Business Writing

Writing assignments in business courses may ask students to use specific formats for memos, letters, and reports.

Memos and Letters

Memos are used to communicate with associates within the organization. Letters are used to communicate with associates, clients, and customers outside the organization. The messages of memos and letters can be divided roughly into three types: pleasant, unpleasant, and persuasive. Pleasant memos are usually developed deductively; that is, the main message is stated first, details about the main message are related in the second paragraph, and socially appropriate comments bring the message to a conclusion. Usually, the active voice is used for pleasant messages.

Unpleasant and persuasive messages are usually developed inductively; that is, the writer tries to establish rapport in the first paragraph, introduce the topic in the second, relate the unpleasant message or request in the third or fourth, and close on common ground in the last. Frequently, the passive voice is used to distance the writer from the unpleasant message.

The tone of the memo or letter depends on the relationship between the writer and the intended reader, the purpose of the message, and the expected attitude of the intended reader to the message.

Reports

Reports take a variety of forms determined by their purpose. Some are informational, some are analytical, and some are persuasive. Annual, procedural, and progress reports convey information. Evaluation reports analyze and pass judgment. Justification and recommendation reports and proposals aim to persuade.

One type of specialized report is the marketing plan. It follows a format similar to the marketing planning outline below.

Strategic Marketing Planning Outline

   I. Executive Summary
  II. The Business Opportunity
      A.   The Core Product / Service Concept
 III. Situation Analysis
      A.   Organizational Mission, Goals, and Objectives
      B.   Resources Required
 IV. Marketing Action Plan
      A.   Overview of the Industry
      B.   Macro Environment Factors
      C.   Organizational Strengths / Weaknesses
      D.   Competitors' Strengths / Weaknesses
      E.   Marketing Goals and Objectives
      F.   Marketing Research Results Recommendations
      G.   Market Segmentation
      H.   Target Market Selection
      I.   Product Positioning

Conventions of Style and Format

Because time is money for both the writer and the reader, business writing is clear and concise. Memos and letters do not take more than one page without a good reason.

Every part of a business document conveys a message: the paper, the letterhead, the print, the placement on the page, the organization, the words and phrasing of the message, and the spelling and punctuation. High-quality stationery and print imply that the business is prosperous and that the sender may have a high position in the organization. Aesthetically pleasing placement of type on the page and well-chosen words and flawless mechanics convey an image of competence and are expected in all business correspondence. A client receiving a letter from an accountant with errors in spelling or punctuation may begin to question the accuracy of the accountant's figures.

Paragraphs and sentences in business memos are usually kept short. Although the purpose and intended reader determine the length of both, between four and eight lines is recommended. Frequently, a paragraph in a letter or memo may have only one or two sentences. Because reading difficulty is determined by length of sentences and number of difficult words (words of three or more syllables according to the Gunning-Fog Index), sentences should be kept under 20 words in length.

When important information can be listed, it is usually listed with each item preceded by a bullet, dash, asterisk, or numeral. This format enables the reader to find the information quickly on the first reading and again when using the letter for reference or responding.

Memos and Letters

Because memos travel within an organization, they have a simple heading, which is frequently printed for use by the company. This heading includes the following components:

To:

From:

Date:

Re:

Although the order of these items may vary, the items themselves are standard. They are placed about an inch from the top of the page or two spaces below the letterhead if letterhead paper is used. Because a memo's message begins two or three spaces below its heading, the memo usually does not look centered on the page.

A business letter should look centered on the page, slightly higher rather than lower. The lines of paragraphs should be single-spaced with double-spacing between the paragraphs. The first word of each paragraph may be indented, but the trend is to start each line at the left margin. Other trends are as follows:

- To omit *dear* in the salutation when the writer does not know the reader
- To omit the salutation and complimentary close if the name of the reader is not known
- To use *attention* and *subject* lines especially when the salutation is being omitted

Remember, time is money. Businesses want to save time in both producing and reading correspondence. Aesthetic appeal communicates prosperity and competence. Do not underestimate the importance of either in writing for business.

Reports

A report may be considered formal or informal depending on the number of supplementary parts, which tend to increase as the length of the body of the report increases. A formal report may have a cover; title fly sheet; title page; table of contents; table of figures; letter of transmittal; glossary; endnotes; works cited; or references; and appendices.

- The **title fly** is a blank sheet of paper placed between the cover and title page in the most formal reports.

- The **title page** gives the title, names(s) of the intended reader(s), name(s) of the sender(s), and date of completion.

- The **table of contents** lists the internal headings of the body of the report and the supplementary parts in the order in which they appear and the numbers of the pages on which they begin.

- The **letter of transmittal** addresses the intended reader, the person who authorized the production of the report. It responds to the letter of authorization and tells what the writers did and how they did it.

- The **summary** contains the main points of the report in less than a page. Some departments, such as engineering, like them even shorter. If readers being addressed by the document are in higher management, the summary is called the "Executive Summary." Executive Summaries are extremely important in business because many busy executives may have time to read only this summary. Summaries of highly technical reports are frequently written in lay language.

- The **body** typically introduces its parts with internal headings. The subjects and order of these parts are determined pragmatically. However, the most important facts usually come first to save time for the reader.

- The **glossary** defines any words that some of the intended readers may need to have defined.

- The **appendix** includes any supporting materials that are referenced in the text: tables, charts, graphs, contracts, photographs, maps, floor plans, graphic illustrations, graphic exhibits, questionnaires, and pictures. Each item in an appendix should have a title. A report may have more than one appendix when need demands more.

Students writing business reports commonly feel uncomfortable with the overlapping of information in the letter of transmittal, the summary, and the introduction and conclusion of the body. True, these parts overlap, but each is there for a different purpose and a different intended reader. Some readers need to be familiar with the general scope of the report but do not have to know the details. They read the summary only. Other readers must know the details. They read the whole report. In highly technical reports that must be read by managers who do not know the technical language, summaries are written in language appropriate for these readers.

Case Studies

Case studies are specialized reports in business. The case study method is an important business tool because it allows the simulation of actual managerial experience through problem analysis, discussion, and decision-making activities. By participating in this simulated management process, you will learn to apply logical, systematic thinking processes to diagnose problems and recommend solutions. One of the main objectives of writing case studies is developing a logical argument and employing a clear and concise train of thought.

The format of case studies in business is similar to those in other disciplines such as the social sciences. Please refer to the case study section in the social sciences on page 118 for further information on case studies.

Documentation Formats

Because many institutions and industrial organizations publish their own documentation manuals, formats vary in this discipline more than in the others discussed in this book. If the employer specifies an in-house or other format, the writer must follow it. However, if no style is specified, the writer may choose from a number of recommended styles, such as MLA, APA, or Chicago format.

In any case, information is cited in the text, in footnotes, in endnotes, or in works cited or reference supplements in accordance with the chosen format.

Sample Student Papers in Business

Three student reports follow: an analysis, a proposal, and a solution to a statistical problem. The analysis draws from secondary research and uses the MLA format. The proposal relies on primary research which is documented in the text.

The example of a statistical assignment uses *Minitab* (a statistical software program) for confidence intervals and hypothesis testing. There are two versions of the report. One is a short version with simple *Minitab* data output. The longer version includes *Minitab* histograms. The assignments are identical except that alpha is set at .01 in the shorter version and .05 in the longer version. Since students are allowed to select the test statistic, the reports use brackets to enclose the *optional* test statistics and test statistic results. An actual report would utilize only *one* of the options.

Sample Business Paper
Analysis of a Company
MLA Style

An Analysis of

the Growth Potential of

Candela Laser Corporation

for

Dr. Richard Maxell

Bay State Eye and Health Care

Weymouth, Massachusetts

by

Janet Sheehan

Financial Consultant

ABC Financial Consultants

November 4, 1988

ii

Bay State Eye and Health Care
320 Washington Street
Suite 205 Weymouth, MA 02186
September 30, 1988

Janet Sheehan
ABC Financial Consultants
500 River Street
Braintree, MA 02184

Dear Ms. Sheehan:

I would like you to prepare a report about
Candela Laser Corporation that will assist me
in my decision to buy stock.

I would like you to research the financial
statements of 1987 and 1988.

Specifically, I would like you to research the
growth potential of Candela Laser Corporation
and recommend whether or not to make an
investment.

As you know, Candela Laser Corporation is
planning a public stock offering on November 15,
1988. From the outside, Candela appears to have
an excellent growth potential. But we all know
that every good investment decision is backed by
hours of research on the inside operations of a
corporation. I will base my decision on your
report and recommendation.

You can call me at (617) 337-1234 to discuss
your fees. Please have this report in my office
by November 5, 1988.

Sincerely,

Richard Maxell, Ph. D.

iii

ABC Financial Consultants
500 River Street
Braintree, MA 02184
November 4, 1988

Dr. Richard Maxell
Bay State Eye and Health Care
Suite 205
Weymouth, MA 02186

Dear Dr. Maxell:

Here is the report about Candela Laser
Corporation that you requested.

The report focuses on the growth potential of
Candela Laser Corporation based on an analysis
of the 1987 and 1988 financial statements.

After extensive research on the above financial
statements, I have concluded that Candela Laser
Corporation is violating Statement of Financial
Accounting Standards 48, which deals with
revenue recognition. This raises the question
of whether Candela Laser Corporation can
continue doing business. I recommend that
you do not participate in Candela Laser
Corporation's public stock offering.

If you have any questions, please do not
hesitate to call me at (617) 843-1234,
extension 21.

Sincerely,

Janet Sheehan

Janet Sheehan

iv

CONTENTS

v

Summary

Candela Laser Corporation began by developing scientific lasers and now develops dermatology and urology lasers as well.

Candela tripled its sales in one quarter and turned its loss of $1.3 million into a profit of $727,000 in one year, due to its sales of dermatology and urology lasers. But while doing so, it violated Statement of Financial Accounting Standards 48, "Revenue Recognition When Right of Return Exists."

The result of that violation decreases the 1988 reported profit of $727,000 to a loss of almost $2 million.

Due to high marketing and developing costs associated with this industry and the loss in 1988, Candela Laser Corporation may not be able to continue doing business in the future. Therefore I recommend that you do not participate in the November 15, 1988, public stock offering.

1

INTRODUCTION

Candela Laser Corporation was founded in
1970 by two physicists, Horace Furumoto and
Harry Ceccon. From 1970 to 1980, Candela
Laser Corporation developed scientific lasers
and sold them to universities and federal
agencies. Sales were less than $1 million
per year.

In 1981, Candela began to develop
dermatology and urology lasers. To market the
lasers, Candela raised $4.2 million in a June
1986 public stock offering at $3 per share.
Late in 1986, Candela began to market both
lasers. In April of 1987, Candela began to
ship its urology laser. In June 1987, Candela
raised another $5 million in a private
offering of their stock. In March 1988,
Candela shipped its dermatology laser. By
June 30, 1988, medical laser systems
accounted for 68% of Candela's sales.
According to Richard J. Olsen, the chief
financial officer, Candela believes that
its dermatology laser alone will bring in
$60 million over the next five years (Fitz
Simon 38).

In April 1988, Candela received The New
Englander Award, issued annually by the Small
Business Association of New England, Inc.
(Fitz Simon 38).

Candela is already researching developing
lasers to treat eye diseases and to blast
plaque from clogged arteries (Fitz Simon 38).

2

THE PROBLEM

Financial Statement Analysis

As Figure 1 shows, in the first three quarters of the year ended June 30, 1987, Candela suffered losses due to high marketing costs. Then in the last quarter, as Candela began to ship its urology laser, sales almost tripled, resulting in a profit of $108,000. But overall, for the year ended June 30, 1987, Candela suffered a loss of $1.3 million.

For the year ended June 30, 1988, the year during which Candela began shipping its dermatology laser, Candela reported a profit of $727,830.

Figure 1

Candela's Condensed Financial Statements (000)

quarter ended---	9/30/86	12/31/86	3/31/87	6/30/87	Total
sales	$ 943	$ 799	$1,010	$2,900	$5,552
expenses	1,051	1,903	1,644	2,792	6,890
profit/ loss	$ (208)	$ (604)	$(634)	$ 108	$(1,338)

quarter ended---	9/30/87	12/31/87	3/31/88	6/30/88	Total
sales	$2,800	$3,100	$3,910	$5,970	$15,780
expenses	2,642	3,264	3,758	5,389	15,053
profit/ (loss)	$ 158	$ (164)	$ 152	$ 581	$ 727

Source: Wall Street Journal Quarterly Earnings Digest

3

It is very unusual for any company to turn a $1.3 million loss into a $727,000 profit in one year. After further analysis of the notes to the financial statements, specifically the one cited in Exhibit 1, I have found that Candela is violating the revenue recognition policy, resulting in incorrect sales figures and an overstatement of income.

<u>Revenue Recognition</u>

The basic concept of revenue recognition is to recognize revenue when it is earned, realized, and recognizable or when the product is substantially completed and shipped to the customer. Candela Laser Corporation completed its lasers and shipped them to their customers, justifying revenue recognition according to the basic concept as shown in Exhibit 1. But many of Candela's "customers" included independent distributors who had the right to return the lasers (Fitz Simon 71). A sale with the right to return is one of the exceptions to the basic concept.

Candela has violated SFAS 48, "Revenue Recognition When Right of Return Exists." Candela had sold many of its lasers to independent distributors who retained the right to return the lasers if they were unable to sell to hospitals, clinics, or doctors.

Under SFAS 48, six requirements must be met in order to count the sale as revenue at the point of sale. The six requirements are shown in Exhibit 2. If not all the requirements are met, revenue cannot be recognized until the right to return provision expires.

4

One of the requirements is that the buyer, the independent distributors in this case, be indebted to the seller and the indebtedness not be contingent on the resale of the merchandise. Candela has stated that payment from the distributors is dependent on the resale of the system (Fitz Simon 71). Therefore, Candela does not meet this requirement.

Another requirement is that a reasonable estimate can be made of future returns that will be allowed. According to Martin Miller, author of <u>GAAP Guide</u>, SFAS 48 cites the following factors that decrease the possibility of making a reasonable estimate:

1. Possible technical obsolescence or change in demand for merchandise
2. Little or no experience in determining returns for specific types of merchandise

Laser technology is a rapidly changing technology. Therefore, technical obsolescence is possible. As a matter of fact, another one of Candela's problems is that it had technically obsolete inventory. This would lead to decreasing the possibility of making a reasonable estimate. Also, medical lasers are fairly new technology. Candela has not had the experience required to determine an estimate of the returns. Candela has not met the requirement of making a reasonable estimate of future returns.

5

CONCLUSION

Although laser technology has a promising future, that future is not with Candela Laser Corporation.

After analyzing revenue transactions more carefully, I have concluded that since Candela did not meet the requirements of SFAS 48, Candela could not report certain sales as revenues. The sales that Candela should not have reported amount to approximately $2.7 million in 1988. This would have left Candela suffering a loss of about $2 million instead of a profit of $727,000 in 1988. This restatement is shown in Figure 2. Because of the high marketing and developing costs that any company in the medical laser field must face, I have serious doubts that Candela can continue doing business in the future. Therefore I recommend that you do not participate in the November 15, 1988, public stock offering.

Figure 2

Candela's 1988 Financial Statement Restated (000)

sales	$13,080
expenses	15,053
profit/(loss)	$(1,973)

6

<u>**Exhibit 1**</u>
<u>Candela Laser Corporation</u>
<u>Excerpts from Notes to Financial Statements</u>
<u>For Year Ended June 30, 1987</u>

<u>Revenue Recognition</u>

Generally, the Company recognizes revenue as completed machines are shipped to customers.

7

Exhibit 2

Summary of the Provisions of SFAS 48

When a buyer has the right to return merchandise purchased, the seller may not recognize income from the sale, unless all of the following conditions are met:

1. The price between the seller and the buyer is substantially fixed or determinable.

2. The seller has received full payment, or the buyer is indebted to the seller and the indebtedness is not contingent on the resale of the merchandise.

3. Physical destruction, damage, or theft of the merchandise would not change the buyer's obligation to the seller.

4. The buyer has economic substance and does not exist solely for the benefit of the seller.

5. No significant obligations exist for the seller to help the buyer resell the merchandise.

6. A reasonable estimate can be made of the amount of future returns.

8

Works Cited

Fitz Simon, Jane. "Lasers Glow Like Gold at Candela." <u>The Boston Globe</u>, 10 May 1988: 33+.

---."Audit Problem Stops Candela's Public Offering." <u>The Boston Globe</u>, 2 November 1988: 71+

Miller, Martin. <u>GAAP Guide</u>. New York: HBJ, 1990.

Sample Business Paper
Proposal

Proposal:

Raising Telephone Rates at

The City View Hotel

Nicole Gallant

Prof. Polanski

Writing for Business

April 28, 1992

ii

Mr. Michael da Silva
City View Hotel
104 Lobster Lane
Bayview, SC 04596

April 16, 1992

Dear Michael:

Here is the report about raising the current
telephone charges at the City View Hotel.
I surveyed several of the local Bayview
hotels and discovered that the City View
charges lower rates in the following areas:

1. Local calls
2. Long distance markup
3. 1-800 calls
4. Directory assistance
5. Pay stations

Using these results as the basis, I propose
the following increases:

1. Local calls by $.15
2. Long distance markup by 9.4%
3. 1-800 calls by $.75
4. Directory assistance by $.15
5. Pay stations by 20%

These proposed increases would significantly
increase telephone revenue. Hotel profit
would rise by an estimated $108,666.00
annually. This is a great way for the hotel
to earn a larger profit. This added profit
would allow the hotel to improve the current
services offered to guests and to find more
ways to satisfy guest and employee needs.

As you requested, a copy of this report was
sent to Mr. Alan and Mr. Michael Spaulding.

Sincerely,

Nicole Gallant

Nicole Gallant

iii

Ms. Nicole Gallant
City View Hotel
104 Lobster Lane
Bayview, SC 04596

March 16, 1992

Dear Nicole:

Please write a report proposing an increase
in the hotel's current telephone charges.
It has come to my attention that the City
View Hotel charges the guests below average
rates for local, long distance, and credit
card calls. An increase in these charges
could be very profitable for the hotel.

This report should include the average rate
charged to guests by local Bayview hotels,
an estimate of increase needed to bring
rates to the average, and graphs showing
the forecasted profit that will result
from an increase.

Please finish this report by April 16, 1992.
Send copies of the finished report to the
hotel owners Mr. Alan and Mr. Michael
Spaulding. Thank you for your time and help.

Sincerely,

Michael da Silva

Michael da Silva

iv

TABLE OF CONTENTS

v

TABLE OF FIGURES

EXECUTIVE SUMMARY

The City View Hotel charges below average
telephone rates. This report proposes
increases in the following areas:

1. Local calls
2. Long distance markup
3. 1-800 calls
4. Directory assistance
5. Pay stations

These increases would help the hotel
generate an estimated profit of $807,415
annually. This would mean that there would
be an increase in current telephone revenue
of $108,666. These figures are based on the
average number of calls made by hotel guests
during the past year.

1

INTRODUCTION

One way for the City View Hotel to compete
better with local hotels is to raise
telephone rates. Currently the City View
charges telephone rates that are below the
average charged by the surrounding hotels.

Increasing the telephone rates at the City
View to meet the average of the local hotels
will mean a greater revenue. This increased
revenue will allow the hotel to spend more
money on improving guest services. This
improvement would ensure guest satisfaction,
return visits, and a better all-around
reputation for the City View. This would
also increase hotel revenue because guests
would return to the hotel and recommend the
City View to their friends and business
associates.

SURVEY

Hotels surveyed:
Ten local Bayview hotels were surveyed in
order to prepare this report. Following is a
list of the hotels that were involved in the
survey.

1. City View Hotel

2. Seaview Inn

3. Hill Crest Hotel

4. Drop Inn

5. Bay Towers

   6. Edelweiss Lodge

   7. Fieldbrook House

   8. The White Hart

   9. The Castle

10. The Gatehouse

Method:
A call-around was conducted to survey the
hotels listed above. I called each of these
hotels and spoke with the Communications
Manager or the Front Desk Manager. Some of
the smaller hotels did not have a specific
Communications Manager.

I questioned each manager about his or her
telephone charges in each of the following
areas:

1. Local calls

2. Long distance markup

3. Access charge for credit cards

4. 1-800 calls

5. 1-900, 1-950, & 1-550 calls

6. Directory assistance

7. Pay stations

3

Results:

Figure 1

TELEPHONE CHARGE SURVEY

	City View Hotel	Seaview Inn	Hill Crest Hotel	Drop Inn	Bay Towers
Local calls	$.60	$.75	$.75	$.60	$.90
Long distance markup	32%	30%	38%	35%	--
Access charge credit cards	$.75	$.75	$.75	$.65	--
1-800 calls	$.00	$.00	$.75	$.00	--
1-900, 1-950, 1-550 calls	NO	NO	NO	NO	--
Pay stations	14%	20%	25%	20%	--
Directory assistance	$.60 local $.75 long distance	$.75	$.75	$.75	--

	Edelweiss Lodge	Fieldbrook House	The White Hart	The Castle	The Gate-house
Local calls	$.80	$.60	$.90	$.75	$.85
Long distance markup	92%	35%	99%	40%	50%
Access charge credit cards	$.92	$.75	$1.00	$1.00	$.00
1-800 calls	$.92	$.75	$.90	$.75	$.00
1-900, 1-950, 1-550 calls	NO	NO	NO	YES $5.00	NO
Pay stations	15%	20%	25%	20%	20%
Directory assistance	$.92	$.60	$ .50	$.75	$.85

4

Problems with the survey:

The Bay Towers refused to participate in the whole survey and answered only the first question. The manager said it was illegal for them to give out the hotel charges for telephone rates. After talking with several of our managers and law consultants, I verified that the Bay Towers was incorrect. It is not illegal for hotels to disclose their telephone charges to outside sources or guests. If a guest disputes a bill, that guest has a right to know what he is being charged for. The Bay Towers is one of the most expensive and exclusive hotels in the city; it probably wants to maintain this image by refusing to participate in this survey.

Discussion of results:

1.   Local calls
The City View charges $.60 for local calls. On the average this is $.15 less than the surrounding Bayview hotels. The range of charges for this fee is from $.60 to $.90. The City View falls at the very bottom of the scale.

2.   Long distance markup
The City View also falls at the bottom of the scale in this category. Our hotel currently marks up long distance phone calls by 32%. This is three points less than that charged by the two other Spaulding hotels. The more expensive hotels, like the Bay Towers and The White Hart, affected the average because their markups are

5

90%-99%. The average for the local hotels that
fall in the same price range as the City View
is 39%.

3.   Access charge for credit cards
All the hotels surveyed, except The Gatehouse,
charge a fee for using credit cards. The
average for this fee is $.73. The City View is
above average by $.02.

4.   1-800 calls
Through this survey it was discovered that the
local hotels are beginning to charge a hook-up
fee for 1-800 phone calls. The majority of the
hotels that charge for this service use the
same amount for this fee as they do for local
calls. This is due to the fact that the hook-up
fee charged to the hotel by the phone company
for 1-800 calls is the same as that for local
calls. If the hotels do not charge the guests
for these calls, they will lose money because
they are still responsible for paying the phone
company. The hotels that already charge for
this service have seen an increase in revenue.
The average for this fee is $.81, and the City
View currently falls way below average because
it does not charge for this service.

5.   1-900, 1-950, 1-550 calls
Of all the hotels surveyed, only The Castle
allows 1-900 calls to be made from the guest
rooms. The Castle charges $5.00 for these calls.

6

The City View falls in line with the other
hotels by restricting 1-900 calls. This
restriction means that guests are not allowed
to make 1-900 calls from their rooms.

6. Pay stations
The average markup for pay stations is 20%.
This puts the City View below average by 6
points because the current markup is 14%.

7. Directory assistance
Through this survey it was discovered that
the City View is the only hotel that charges
different rates for local and long distance
directory assistance. The City View charges
$.60 for local directory assistance and $.75
for long distance directory assistance. The
average for this fee is $.71. The City View
is below average for local calls and above
average for long distance calls.

PROPOSED INCREASES
As a result of this survey, I propose that
the hotel increase its telephone charges in
the following areas:

1. Local calls

2. Directory assistance

3. 1-800 calls

4. Long distance markup

5. Pay stations

7

Local calls: (see figure 2)
This fee should be raised by $.15 in order
for our prices to meet the average of the
local Bayview hotels.

Directory assistance: (see figure 2)
This fee should be consistent for local and
long distance directory assistance. This
consistency can be created by increasing the
charge for local directory assistance to
$.75. By increasing this charge, the three
Spaulding hotels will have uniformed rates.

1-800 calls: (see figure 2)
Since most hotels in this area are beginning
to charge for 1-800 calls, I propose that
the City View also instate this fee. It
would be appropriate to charge $.75 for this
service because $.75 will cover the cost of
connecting the quest to an outside line.

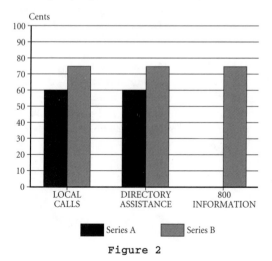

Figure 2

8

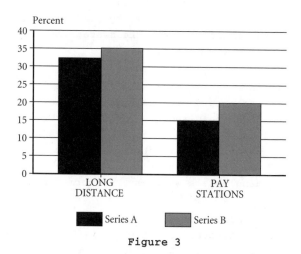

Figure 3

Long distance markup: (see figure 3)
I propose that the City View raise its
markup to 35% in order to unify the three
Spaulding hotels and have them all charge
the same rate. This will also bring the City
View closer to the average rate.

Pay stations: (see figure 3)
The markup for the pay stations at the City
View is currently below average. I propose
that this percentage be raised to 20% in
order for the hotel to measure up with the
going rates.

9

FORECASTED PROFIT FOR EACH INCREASE

The following forecasted increases are based
on the number of calls made from the City
View Hotel last year.

Local calls:
With an increase of $.15 for local calls the
hotel will earn a net increase of $29,908.75.

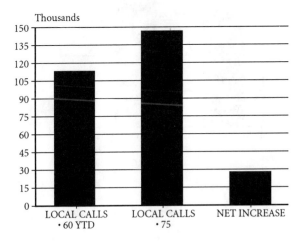

INCREASE OF $28,908.75

PERCENT OF CHANGE 25%   Series A

Figure 4

10

Directory assistance:
Increasing the charge for local directory
assistance phone calls to $.75 will increase
hotel profit by $1,620.00.

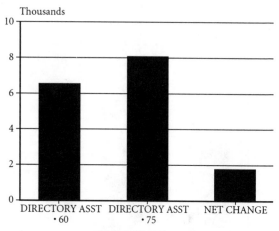

Figure 5

11

1-800 calls:
Instating a new charge of $.75 for 1-800
calls will increase hotel profit by
$13,500.00.

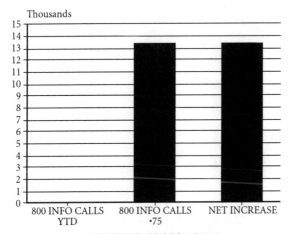

Thousands

NET INCREASE OF $13,500.00

BASED ON 1500 CALLS PER MONTH   Series A

Figure 6

12

Long distance markup:
By increasing the long distance markup to 35%
the hotel will earn a net increase of
$52,675.22.

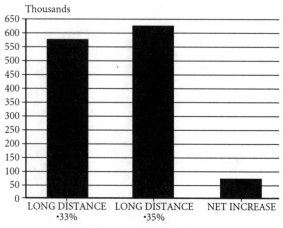

Figure 7

13

Pay stations:
An increase in the markup for pay stations to
20% will increase hotel profit by $4,483.71.

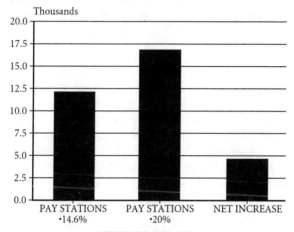

Figure 8

14

FORECASTED REVENUE

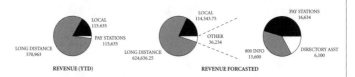

Figure 9

The telephone revenue year to date is equal
to $698,749.00, which is a good amount for
the size of this hotel. However, these slight
increases in rates will greatly increase
annual revenue by $108,666.00. Using the
number of phone calls made by guests last
year, we project an annual revenue of
$807,415.00.

15

BENEFITS OF THESE INCREASES

As a result of these increases, the City View
will receive many benefits. First and most
important is the increase in hotel revenue.
With this new revenue the hotel will have an
opportunity to satisfy guests and employee
needs more efficiently. There are many areas
where this money could be used to improve the
hotel. The money will not pay for all of
these, but the suggestions are as follows:

1. Renovate the guest rooms. The monthly
comment cards reveal that the guests are
dissatisfied with the noise level of the
hotel and the heating units. This extra money
could be used to discover ways to soundproof
the rooms. Because the City View is such an
old hotel, the heating system is also very
old. This money could be put to updating this
system so that the guest rooms are not
extremely hot or cold. This regulation of
temperature would make the guests happier,
improve the comments on the comment cards,
and make guests more willing to return to
the hotel and recommend this hotel to their
friends.

2. Hire more bellmen. Lack of bellmen is
another common complaint on the comment
cards. Due to the economy the City View has
had to cut back on help. This added revenue
could be used to invest in more bellmen. This
increase of staff would make check-in go
smoother and faster. The guests would be
happier because they would have quicker

service getting to their room, and the guest
service agents would be happier because they
would not have to listen to guests yell at
them as a result of a short bell staff.
Comment cards would also improve because
guests would be happier.

3. Create more hotel advertisements. By
spending more money on advertising, the name
and reputation of our hotel would reach more
people worldwide. This outreach will attract
more travelers and also increase hotel
profit. The more a person hears the name of
a hotel the more interested he or she is to
stay at the hotel.

4. Buy new uniforms for hotel employees. This
step would please employees by giving them
a little extra boost, and it may make them
happier with their job to know that they are
being thought of by the management.

5. Give raises to hard-working hotel
employees. There are many dedicated employees
who are becoming dissatisfied with the hotel
because they are not receiving the
appreciation that they deserve.

6. Set up a day-care service for employees
and guests. This convenience would make life
easier for the employees who have small
children and find it difficult to work and
raise a family. This service could also be
offered to guests traveling with children

17

who may want to go out for a night on the
town and to leave the little ones at home.

7. Set up a service for employees with the
surrounding garages which would allow
employees to park in a garage for a lower
rate. This arrangement would make an easier
and more pleasant commute for many employees
who have difficulty using public
transportation due to their work schedules.

Sample Business Paper
Statistical Report for Management

Quantitative   Professor Annie Puciloski
Analysis 11-BA206   Duffy 217E
Minitab Assignment #3   apuciloski@stonehill.edu

Prepare a Report for management on the
following business problem:

[Length to be determined by information to be
reported. Minitab output to be included as
needed for clarification]

We are *ClipIt!*, Inc., a manufacturer of
paperclips. Our line of standard, small,
silver clips are packed in 250-count boxes.
We have designed and calibrated our two-shift
operation fill-line equipment to fill an
average, μ 268 clips per box with a standard
deviation, σ of 8 clips. We take random
samples during the first and last hour of
each shift to determine whether the fill-line
equipment is operating properly in regards to
average paperclips per box. By aiming to fill
268 clips on average, we minimize the
probability of filling less than the labeled
250-count.

The fill-line observation data is in the
Minitab "PaperClips" Worksheet. Sample 1 and
Sample 2 are the first and last hour samples
for Shift 1; Sample 3 and Sample 4 are the
first and last hour samples for Shift 2 taken
today. We set alpha, α at .05.

INFORMATION TO BE INCLUDED IN YOUR REPORT TO
MANAGEMENT:

1. Maximum Sampling Error.

2. Confidence Interval estimates about the
   sample means (x-bars)

3. Statements about these Confidence Interval
   estimates.

   [include <u>identification</u> of the <u>actual</u>
   <u>population</u> as well as the <u>population</u>
   <u>parameter</u> being estimated.]

4. Hypothesis tests about the population mean
   for each sample

   Hypothesis tests should include
   —proper Form of the test and explanation
    about Form selection

   —Test statistic, i.e. the critical-value
    statistic for your Rejection Rule
    (<u>YOUR</u> choice!)

   —Rejection Rule

   —sample statistic comparison to
    critical-value statistic

   —statistical conclusion

   —your action-recommendation to management
    in regards to the fill-line operation

[NOTE: we take <u>each</u> sample, <u>then</u> conclude from
<u>each</u> hypothesis test whether the fill-line is
functioning properly.]

ClipIt! Quality Department
Daily Sampling Analysis Report
May 20th
prepared by Gwendolyn G. Alphonse

As a function of sample size, *n*, 64, and
Confidence Level, 95%, our Sampling Error
indicates that there is a 95% chance that an
interval estimate of the population mean
number of paperclips per box will provide a
maximum Sampling Error of no more than 1.96
paperclips, based on *any* randomly selected
sample of 64 observations. (See Endnote 1)

Our 95% Confidence Intervals are constructed
by adding and subtracting 1.96 paperclips to
each randomly selected sample mean number of
paperclips per box. We can state that each
interval estimate of μ (actual mean number of
paperclips per box) will be accurate to
within plus or minus 1.96 paperclips of the
sample mean number of paperclips per box.

Our hypothesis tests, conducted on each
Shift's first and last hour's randomly
selected sample, test for the population mean
being not equal to the hypothesized mean of
260 paperclips.

H_o: $\mu = 260$

H_a: $\mu \neq 260$

These are two-tail test because we do not
want to either underfill or overfill.
Underfilling subjects us to the possibility
of filling less than the labeled 250-count,
and overfilling could result in serious
fill-line problems and possible production
shut-down. With alpha set at .05, we incur
a 5% risk of committing a Type I (false

negative) Error if we reject the null hypothesis based on our random sampling.

Our Rejection Rule is [either]
Reject the null if critical x-bar (sample mean) < 266.04 or > 269.96 paperclips per box (See Endnote #2.)

[or]   Reject the null if sample p-value < .01 (See Endnote #3.)

[or]   Reject the null if sample Z_{score} < -1.96 or > +1.96 (*See* Endnote #4.)

Sampling Results for May 19th attached herewith.

Sampling Results for May 19th
Minitab *output data imported into this document, highlighted for clarity.*

Shift 1: Sample 1 taken first hour

Confidence Intervals
The assumed sigma = 8.00

Variable	N	Mean	StDev	SE Mean	**95.0 % CI**
Sample 1	64	267.61	9.01	1.00	**(265.03, 270.19)**

We were 99% confident that the actual population mean number of paperclips per box fell between 265.03 and 270.19 paperclips.

Z-Test
Test of mu = 268.00 vs mu not = 268.00
The assumed sigma = 8.00

Variable	N	**Mean**	StDev	SE Mean	**z**	**P**
Sample 1	64	**267.61**	9.01	1.00	**-0.39**	**0.70**

Since Sample *x*-bar (sample mean), 267.61 >
265.43 and < 270.57 we could not reject the null
[Likewise, our Sample p-value, .70 > .01 and our
Sample Z_{score}, -.39 > -2.57 and < +2.57.]
hypothesis and concluded that the fill-line was
functioning normally. We continued operations.

Shift 1: Sample 2 taken last hour

Confidence Intervals
The assumed sigma = 8.00

Variable	N	Mean	StDev	SE Mean	**95.0 % CI**
Sample 2	64	269.25	8.75	1.00	**(266.67, 271.83)**

**We were 99% confident that the actual population
mean number of paperclips per box fell between
266.67 and 271.83 paperclips.**

Z-Test
Test of mu = 268.00 vs mu not = 268.00
The assumed sigma = 8.00

Variable	N	**Mean**	StDev	SE Mean	**Z**	**P**
Sample 2	4	**269.25**	8.75	1.00	**1.25**	**0.21**

Since Sample *x*-bar (sample mean), 269.25 > 265.43
and < 270.57 we could not reject the null
[Likewise, our Sample p-value, .21 >.01 and our
Sample Z_{score}, 1.25 > -2.57 and < +2.57.]
hypothesis and concluded the fill-line was
functioning normally. We continued operations.

Shift 2 Sample 3 taken first hour

Confidence Intervals
The assumed sigma = 8.00

Variable	N	Mean	StDev	SE Mean	**95.0 % CI**
Sample 3	64	271.08	10.41	1.00	**(268.50, 273.65)**

We were 99% confident that the actual population mean number of paperclips per box fell between 268.50 and 273.65 paperclips.

Z-Test
Test of mu = 268.00 vs mu not = 268.00
The assumed sigma = 8.00

Variable	N	**Mean**	StDev	SE Mean	**Z**	**P**
Sample 3	64	**271.08**	10.41	1.00	**3.08**	**0.0021**

Since Sample *x*-bar (sample mean), 271.08 > 265.43 we rejected the null [Likewise, our Sample p-value, .0021 < .01 and our Sample Z_{score}, 3.089 > +2.57.] hypothesis and concluded that the fillline equipment was not functioning normally. We discontinued operations and conducted our normal quality check for deficiencies.

Shift 2: Sample 4 taken last hour

Confidence Intervals
The assumed sigma = 8.00

Variable	N	Mean	StDev	SE Mean	**95.0 % CI**
Sample 4	64	265.52	9.29	1.00	**(262.94, 268.09)**

We were 99% confident that the actual population mean number of paperclips per box fell between 262.94 and 268.09 paperclips.

Z-Test
Test of mu = 268.00 vs mu not = 268.00
The assumed sigma = 8.00

Variable	N	**Mean**	StDev	SE Mean	**Z**	**P**
Sample 4	64	**265.52**	9.29	1.00	**-2.48**	**0.013**

Since Sample *x*-bar (sample mean), 265.52 > 265.43 < 270.57 we could not reject the null [Likewise, our Sample p-value, .013 < .01 and

our Sample Z_{score}, $-2.48 > -2.57$ and $< +2.57$.]
hypothesis and concluded that the fill-line
equipment was functioning normally. We continued
operations.

Endnotes (Sampling Calculations)

1. With α alpha set at .01, our Confidence
   Coefficient is .99. Corresponding Z_{score} is
   2.57. Maximum Sampling Error, $|x\text{-}bar - \mu| =$
   $|Z_{\alpha/2} \, \sigma_{x\text{-}bar}| = 2.57 \, (\sigma/\sqrt{n}) = 2.57(8/8) =$
   $2.57(1) = 2.57$ paperclips.

2. Critical x-bars (lower and upper tail sample
   means) based on +2.57 and -2.57 Critical
   Z_{scores}.

   $$-2.57 = \frac{x\text{-}bar_1 - 268}{8/\sqrt{64}} \quad x\text{-}bar_1 = 265.43$$
   $$\text{paperclips}$$

   and

   $$+2.57 = \frac{x\text{-}bar_2 - 268}{8/\sqrt{64}} \quad x\text{-}bar_2 = 270.57$$
   $$\text{paperclips}$$

3. Critical p-value is always equal to alpha,
   the probability of committing a Type I Error.
   Each Sample p-value is the observed level of
   significance if the null were rejected based
   on that sample's Z_{score}.

4. Critical Z_{score} for hypothesis tests is also
   2.57 because we are conducting two-tail
   tests.

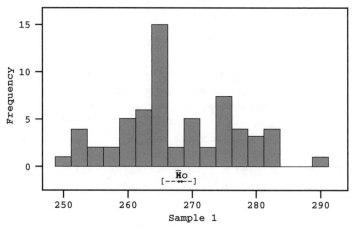

Exhibit 1

Histogram of Sample 1
(with Ho and 95% z-confidence interval
for the mean, sigma = 8.0000)

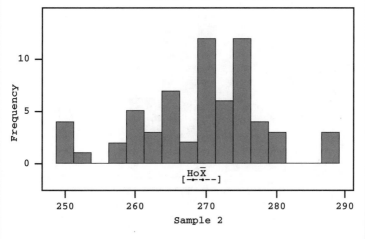

Exhibit 3

Histogram of Sample 3
*(with Ho and 95% z-confidence interval
for the mean, sigma = 8.0000)*

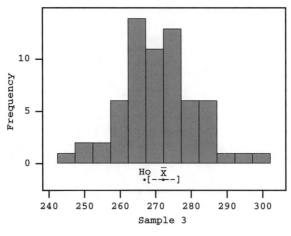

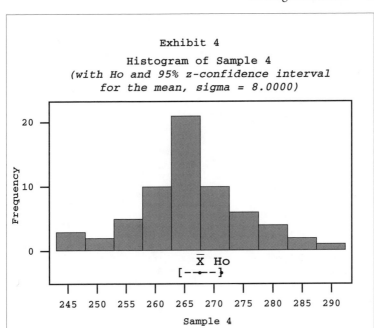

Exhibit 4

Histogram of Sample 4
*(with Ho and 95% z-confidence interval
for the mean, sigma = 8.0000)*

OVERVIEW OF
DOCUMENTATION STYLES: BOOKS

MLA Format (pp. 43–60)   http.//www.mla.org/main_stl.htm

Parenthetical citation in the text

> ... Thoreau's reference to Abraham Lincoln
> (Miller 308).

Work cited at the end of the paper

> Miller, Perry. <u>The American Transcendentalists:
> Their Prose and Poetry</u>. New York: Doubleday,
>   1983.

Chicago Format (pp. 60–65)

Note in the text

> ... acknowledged in 1902 with the
> Hay-Pauncefote Treaties.[1]

Work listed at the end of the paper

Notes:

> 1. David Weigall, <u>Britain and the World:
> 1815-1986</u>. (New York: Oxford University Press,
> 1987), 107.

Bibliography:

> Weigall, David. <u>Britain and the World:
>   1815-1986</u>. New York: Oxford University
>   Press, 1987.

APA Format (pp. 120–128)

Parenthetical citation in the text

> ... a psychological profile of Adolph Hitler
> (Langer, 1972).

Reference at the end of the paper

> Langer, W. C. (1972). <u>The Mind of Adolph Hitler</u>. New York: Basic.

Number-Reference Format (pp. 177–178)

Parenthetical citation in the text

> ... against a living snail has been documented (1, p. 432).

Reference at the end of the paper

> 1.   Barth, R. H.; Broshears, R. E. The invertebrate world. Philadelphia: Saunders College Publishing; 1982.

Name-Year System Format (p. 178)

Parenthetical citation in the text

> ... a small group of proteins are synthesized (Whelan and Hightower, 1985).

Reference at the end of the paper

> Whelan, S. A. and Hightower, L. E. (1985) Differential induction of glucose-regulated and heat shock proteins; effects of pH and sulfhydryl-reducing agents on chicken enbryo cells. <u>J. Cell Phys</u>. 125: 251–258.

OVERVIEW OF
DOCUMENTATION STYLES:
ARTICLES

MLA Format (pp. 43–60)

> LeGuin, Ursula K. "American Science Fiction and
> the Other." <u>Science Fiction Studies</u> 2 (1975):
> 208-10.

Chicago Format (pp. 60–65)

Notes:

> 1. John Huntington, "Science Fiction and
> the Future," <u>College English</u> 37 (Fall 1975):
> 340-58.

Bibliography:

> Huntington, John. "Science Fiction and the
> Future." <u>College English</u> 37 (Fall 1975):
> 340-58.

APA Format (pp. 120–128)

> Miller, W. (1969). Violent crimes in city
> gangs. <u>Journal of Social Issues</u>, 581-593.

Number-Reference Format (pp. 177–178)

> 1.   Cotton, F. A. Photooxidation and photo-
> synthetic pigments. <u>J. Cell Biol</u>. 87:32-43;
> 1987.

Name-Year System Format (p. 78)

> Zishka, M. K. and Nishimura, J. S. (1970) Effect
> of glycerol on Lowry and biuret methods of
> protein determination. <u>Anal Biochem</u>. 34:
> 291-297

INDEX